How God does Change

A thought for every day of the year

Tim Daniel

© 2025 Timothy Daniel
All rights reserved.
NO AI TRAINING
ISBN 979-8-218-81801-2
Library of Congress Control Number: 2025920804
Cover photo by Austin Guhl on Unsplash
First Edition 2025

Acknowledgements

To Dr. Shelly, who somehow knew I would take up the challenge of change.

Prologue

On a short trip we typically designate each day as what the calendar says it is. On a longer and more personal journey it is not uncommon to designate each day cumulatively, by how many days have gone before. This cumulative method conveys the sense of life altering adventure no one else has taken at all or at least not in the same way, rather than an errand taken the same way by everyone. We will use this second method of marking time.

On longer quests there are previously unseen road signs that tell the traveler a landmark lies ahead over the horizon and say, on the left. Road signs serve as placeholders until the landmarks they point toward come into view, then we forget about the signs and remember the landmark instead. For those on long journeys seeing each landmark in the predicted sequence is evidence that 1) the signs were accurate and 2) they are still headed in the right direction. They can keep going with increased confidence in both the journey and the signs. We will use this method of marking progress.

We use road signs to find things that exist, but are at a distance, things we cannot yet see and verify for ourselves. Road signs are important when we must choose to go in one direction or another.

If I believe the road sign, I make a choice and move in the direction it tells me to move. In time I see the landmark for myself. I now know the sign was accurate and dependable. I know someone placed it there for my benefit, while expecting no benefit in return from me.

If on the other hand, the landmark never appears, and I get more frustrated and lost, I don't blame myself for "user error." Rather, I know the sign was in error and I should not have believed its message and will not believe one from the same source in the future.

This book is a series of signs pointing to a sequence of landmarks. The landmarks are real phenomena in history and real relational dynamics going on in, between and around us. The idea of this do-it-yourself guide is to go see for yourself. If what I describe is not there, do not trust it as a guide. Toss it.

If what I describe is there, it might make sense to keep this book around a little longer, but with this caution: At best this book can only point toward a vast reality available to you. This book is not that vast reality. You can find the reality only by entering ethically and directly into the specific, local, and historical situation God gave you and you alone.

No one can do it for you because no one else is you.

I have tried to describe as accurately as I can the sequence of landmarks I encountered as God guided me to enter ever more ethically into direct contact with my own given situation. Those of us who seek God all begin our journeys to God from a different place, but along the way, from different angles and distances, I suspect we will all pass the same types of landmarks. A mirage is a mirage. A log jam is a log jam. An opening is an opening. A river is a river. In each case, once you've seen one, you have a general sense of what to do with the next one you come across. For directional purposes, the larger and older pattern matters more than the small and passing details.

A researcher once tried to train a cat to notice a new toy on the ground. He pointed at the toy and tried to get the cat to look at it. Instead of looking at the toy, the cat kept looking at the tip of his finger, following it wherever it went. The cat was unable to grasp that the finger was not the thing, the finger was merely sending a message about the thing, that a good thing existed that the cat could have enjoyed.

This book exists to indicate that a good thing exists that you can enjoy. The good thing, the way God does change, is available right now in your own, daily situation. It is not here in these pages or in these words. If you can sense I am pointing at something real, put this book down and go look for God.

God will meet you in your concerns, choices, and behaviors, far more vividly and memorably than in these pages.

I have tried to make my words as accurate and thorough as possible. I have made no effort to craft phrases that are smooth, catchy, and quotable. Had I done that, like the confused cat, someone might latch on to my catchy words instead of moving toward the reality they point toward.

Come up with your own words because they will serve you better. You won't forget your own words to describe what you experience when you go see for yourself. Seek and meet God. No one seeks and meets God without being changed on a level beyond words. No one seeks and meets God without eventually becoming a change agent working on God's behalf. We develop a directed working relationship with God, or we have no relationship at all.

A broken world awaits. The journey begins.

Day 1

God does change.

God is the God of change, not the God of permanence.

God does change differently and does a different kind of change.

The difference in God's change will be what ensures the future of life on earth.

Day 2

Change is about doing work that works. Work is using a specific amount of energy for a specific amount of time to displace something from its original state to a new and better state, and in such a way that it does not revert to its original state.

True work moves the needle.

If after a long investment of time and energy the needle didn't move or moved in the opposite direction from the one intended, then the work we did *didn't work*. The change we made didn't really change anything or even made things worse. Few things are more demoralizing than having invested years or decades in an endeavor only to find at the end it functions no better than it did when we started and may even function worse. It is a gut punch.

We have discovered the starting point: We are not God.

We must take this to heart if we are ever to know how God does change. We must first abandon what hasn't worked.

Day 3

This is a journey for those who know firsthand that the way we do change in our lives and in our culture doesn't work. It is not for lack of study, preparation, devotion, determination, or effort. Something else was missing and is still missing. Something vital. Something for which there is no substitute.

And the culture we live in has no idea what it is.

We have reached the second step in the journey: openness.

Day 4

This book is for those who know in their gut something is wrong. We must change the way we go about changing things. We must fix the way we fix things.

What we do know for sure is we don't want to waste the years we have left and get the same results from our efforts as we have been getting.

We know we make resolutions to change and then find ourselves making the same ones again year after year. We sense we can do better but never do better for very long.

It is unwise to depend on what hasn't changed and won't change to change what needs to change. There are some things we can't do by ourselves, yet no other human can help very much because they can't do those things either. We will only mix their confused incompleteness with our own and learn to use their excuses for not really changing that much instead of the ones we used to use.

Something is missing here.

A lot depends on finding what has been missing all along. For all of us. All of humanity is facing losses we aren't prepared to take. Losses from which we may not recover.

We wipe the slate clean and start over.

Day 5

God's work is not about effort that changes nothing. What God does works. What God changes keep changing and grows stronger. What God removes stays gone.

We need a new model for change other than those our culture teaches. Where would we find a solid model of how God does change?

In God's master work.

In nature.

For free.

Day 6

There is no charge for what has been missing all along. The only cost is that you must learn God's way of doing change yourself by doing it. Anyone or who charges you to bring change into your life or organization is itself still part of what hasn't changed in 10,000 years. It can't change itself. It is the very thing that prevents the very changes we most need.

Nature doesn't use consultants or outside experts. All creatures experiencing change in nature do it themselves using information already embedded in them and available around them. So must we. If we do the change ourselves, then we know how to do it again when we need to, how to fix it when it stops working, and how to modify or extend it when needed – all because we chose the parts and arrangement of the parts. This ensures we make a change that can keep changing to fit the situation as it changes.

Nature is not static. Everything continues to change to some degree at some level. Yet certain functions and features remain through all the changes, so much so that when trying to figure out what a creature in the fossil record did to survive millions of years ago we only need to observe the essential functions and features in its closest relative does today to survive.

What is happening now is what was happening then. What is true in natural evolution is true in human history. If the dead don't rise today be assured no one rose from the dead in the past.

That is not how God does change. The Creator did not make a mistake in limiting all creatures to one life and one definitive, final death.

We participate in how God does change by the way we choose to live the one life God gave us as part of the one planet God made that can support our form of life.

Day 7

To learn how God does change, we must first make room to learn. How? By removing things from our lives that take up space but don't change anything for the better. We painfully unlearn false notions of how change works. If the way of doing change we have been using exists nowhere in nature today, and it never existed in nature in any form in the past, it is false.

It is a mirage. Mirages exist in nature and long-lived creatures learn to ignore them.

How do you know you have been following a mirage? You put in all the time, money, and effort, but when you get to your destination what someone promised you is not there. The good things that were supposed to be happening by now are not happening, not really. Often not at all.

Bad things that were not supposed to happen anymore are still happening. New bad things are starting to happen as well. After all this "work," nothing changed for the better, only for the worse.

Others who followed the same path are mad and want someone to blame. They blame each other. If you dare to doubt the veracity of the original promise aloud, they will blame you. They infer surely it is your lack of faith in and commitment to the mirage that caused this failure.

Day 8

When our change efforts don't change anything we want to know what happened. We don't want to repeat such a painful experience. It is natural and healthy to ask, "why didn't it work?"

Those who peddled the mirage in the form of a theory or fable have a standard explanation. You didn't do it right. You didn't do enough of it. You need to purchase the advanced package. You need to hand over more of your life.

Or if it was a group effort – one of you didn't do it right or didn't do enough. You need to hand over more of your organization. You need to punish the laggards, the ones who held things up. Life gets ugly from there.

Day 9

By the time you realize someone has misled you the costs are staggering.

You can't get back the years, the hopes, the energy, the money, or the sense of social safety.

But God is merciful to those who seek genuine and deep correction, no matter how painful or costly it is.

The con artists who fooled you have no mercy. They laughed at you all the way to the bank.

In their plan you get to weep all the way to the grave. They don't plan to attend your funeral. You were just a number, a mark, a convert, a consumer, a voter. They don't even know your name, much less your story.

If this makes you angry, good.

That is what injustice is supposed to do. It means you're still alive and have at least one fight left in you. The fight of your life. The fight for your life. The fight for Life itself.

Anger is an energy source, but it cannot direct itself. When we use anger to direct our efforts we only cause more harm. To be helpful in the fight for Life we must access a source of direction and correction beyond ourselves.

Day 10

God has nothing to do with injustice. Injustice has nothing to do with God. Injustice destroys God's masterpiece: Life itself.

If you want to do change the way God does change, start by having nothing to do with anything that has nothing to do with God's justice.

You have found the third step, another constant in the way God does change: the passionate pursuit of justice – for all of God's creation in all its ever-increasing diversity, everywhere, for all time.

Day 11

God is actively changing our world from one that is unjust and becoming more unjust, to one that constantly becomes more just.

What is justice?

Justice is word we use to describe the set of conditions that allow any creature to become what God intended it to become - so it can perform the function in Creation God created it to perform.

Anything that we do, support, or ignore, that prevents other creatures from fulfilling their God-given purpose, is unjust. If we don't stop these behaviors we will live far from God.

If we live far from God we will never know how God does change.

Day 12

Is there injustice in nature itself? Yes. Among social species there are individuals who signal to their group that there is a predator nearby, when there is none. When the others run for cover, these "dishonest signalers" rush in and gorge themselves on all the available food.

Is there justice in nature when that happens? Yes. Others start to mimic this "dishonest signaling" tactic to get more food. Pretty soon the behavior is widespread. At that point no one believes the "predator nearby" signal when they hear it – even when there truly is a predator approaching.

By misusing something made for the protection of the group, the dishonest signaler has put the whole group in danger and increased the likelihood he himself or his young will become prey.

God's justice falls on entire groups by through natural bad consequences of individual behaviors that the group has allowed to become normal.

Day 13

Any large group includes the innocent - infants, youngsters, elders, the injured, disabled, and the sick. These members are legitimately dependent on the group's care. The group looks after them because they cannot completely look after themselves, whether they want to or not.

When the group fails to stop bad behavior by one of its own, it has started the process of failing to take care of its own.

We can't accept the benefits of being a social special and reject its responsibilities. If we want only the life of a solitary creature we must also accept its perils – no one looks out for us in our time of need.

Day 14

If God intervened and spared the group's helpless ones, the group would learn it does not need to take its social responsibilities seriously, because God will do it for them.

God does not reward social neglect by rescuing us from the consequences of our behaviors. God does not coddle the lazy and cowardly.

Enabling and coddling never changes the world into a more just place. Rather, it makes injustice worse.

God's work only makes things better – for all of Creation.

Day 15

God is the uncreated Creator. The Creator has made a change that is more significant than all other changes combined.

There was once nothing.

Then there was something.

The Creator alone can bring something out of nothing. All other change work uses things that already exist. Only The Creator can bring something into being that never existed before in any form, using no existing resources. Upon that change all subsequent change depends.

The next time you learn about someone who people treat like a god, ask whether he or she has made something from nothing. I don't mean from humble circumstances. I mean from absolutely nothing at all.

Day 16

There is no change agent that compares to God. There is no change agent that we should treat like God – focus on, listen to, mimic, obey, hail as a genius, follow as a savior, trust as a guide.

To learn how God does change we first redirect our constant attention and admiration to the only One who deserves it and keep it there. It is insulting to God to make a passing mention of God every now and then just to cover our bases or to ask for divine assistance twice a year when we get in a jam.

God does not play a bit-part in change. God plays the leading role. We don't. Not any of us.

Day 17

God alone has done something else that is unprecedented and unrivaled. After existence itself, it is the most momentous change that has ever occurred on earth, and perhaps in all the universe.

God made Life out of non-living matter.

Not something life-like. Not a doll or robot that can walk or talk.

Life. Ever changing, ever-adapting, ever ingenious, ever resourceful, ever new Life.

There is nothing artificial about Life's vast intelligence. Life requires no electricity or internet connection to do its work. Life makes no one into a famous billionaire, and makes no nation into a rich empire, as the price of its solutions. Life does not require permission from humans. Life does not take its direction from humans. Life's permission and direction come from God. Life's new creations emerge unnoticed constantly everywhere in response to new conditions.

Since God's changes are small and obscure to begin with, we must be willing to be small and unnoticed if we are to participate in something a new God is doing on earth.

Day 18

Humans have created endless ways to use, exploit, modify, manage, embellish - and kill life. All those activities required life to exist first. But at this writing no one has created life in the lab out of non-living matter.

God alone remains the author of Life. Life stands apart from all other creations. No human author, no matter how wise and helpful, deserves the admiration, attention, and trust that God deserves.

God is the only and final authority that matters when it comes to the things that matter most. We must treat God accordingly if we want to experience how God does change. Otherwise, we're on our own.

God leads. We follow. God corrects. We seek and accept correction. God knows best. We can't.

We don't do change. God changes *us* from the inside out and from the outside in.

Only then can we usefully participate in the changes God's is bringing about on earth.

Day 19

Our first job as humans is to guard life at all costs, because once it is gone we have no ability to bring it back.

Sitting atop the food chain, our lives and civilizations are completely dependent upon Life on earth.

God holds the secrets of life. Clearly we don't.

How can we possibly predict and plan how to save the earth and restore it to its fullness of Life without those secrets in hand? We can't. We won't. Not on our own.

God transfers the secret pathways Life follows to our minds, directly, daily, through unplanned, unforeseen course changes. Any change method that never mentions or cultivates intimacy with and dependence upon God is a food's errand to another mirage.

Very certain and determined people may change their social status from a nobody to a famous somebody by peddling a grand program of transformation, but that is all that will change.

The living systems we depend upon will continue to die.

Day 20

Grand plans, based on the best science available, have a fatal flaw. Plans go unheeded and unfinished because plans and the experts who craft them are powerless to change what must change first – the human heart.

When the heart is hard and cold it can receive nothing. Only God knows know to change the human heart.

Only God can melt the heart of stone, but does not do so a mass scale, using a one-size fits all assembly line. Rather, following the same pattern of adaptation and change that governs all change in nature, God melts one heart at a time, right where it is, unnoticed. God does change by bringing individuals, one at a time, to adjust their behaviors ethically and practically to meet specific situations no one else has experienced.

In nature we find no one-size fits all solutions. Instead, we find ingenious customization on a massive scale.

Day 21

Work that works moves something *from* one condition *to* another condition. God does work that works.

God moves us from false complexity to true complexity. True complexity is what we see in nature. True complexity is the combination of high diversity and high organization.

God works against and changes environments characterized by high uniformity and high organization. God works to destroy all dictatorships, all monocultures. A dictatorship has one answer-giver and one set of answers for everything. A dictatorship can take shape in a friendship, a home, a neighborhood, a religion, a school, a business, a non-profit organization, a political party, a nation.

God places intelligence and adaptability at every level of life. God will not support any form of leadership that ignores that distributed intelligence because it is blind, rigid, and dangerous.

Day 22

God works against and changes environments characterized by high diversity but low cooperation. As a social species we survive and thrive together, or we die out. Because we are all connected.

God works to reign in chaos, to integrate efforts, to focus attention on shared objectives without recourse to bullying, conniving or domination.

God works to limit and harness individual self-interest, not eliminate it. We need a sense of self-preservation and fulfillment. God entrusted that to each of us as a vital resource.

But we also need an equally powerful sense that ultimately we must achieve our highest good together. We learn to always take care of first those things which take care of us all: nature and justice. When those are well-tended to, all of us have a greater chance of preserving and fulfilling the lives which God loaned to us. This allows us to repay what we received and then something more and new, contributing to an ever-greater flourishing of Life on earth.

Day 23

God works against and changes environments of ignorance and rigidity. Complex problems require complex solutions. New problems require new solutions. Fluid problems require fluid solutions.

If I go to a location using an old map and don't find what the map tells me is there my map is wrong. I can't begin adjusting to something I don't see or understand. God does not want us studying only old maps.

God wants us studying current reality until we understand what is really going on. God gave us the powers of observation, experimentation, reason, and cooperative dialogue. God expects us to cultivate and use these faculties to find fresh solutions to what we face today.

Today's situation is never the same as the one we faced ten, twenty, one hundred or two thousand years ago. It is unique in time and location. We are to find justice-producing solutions to today's challenges. If we take on that challenge God will be with us. God will meet us, teach us, and help us.

We become first-hand witnesses to the creative power and genius of God. We will never want to go back to old maps, theories and grand plans from experts who have no direct contact with our situation.

Day 24

God works against and changes environments soaked in magic.

God works against and changes environments soaked in fiction or fantasy.

God does not do magical things. God does not write fiction. God's work is better than all fantasies. To know how God does change we must first show up for work where God does change – in reality. Fiction is to our minds what candy is to our bodies. Reality is to our minds what healthy, natural food is to our bodies. One is a highly processed occasional treat. The other sustains us and keeps us healthy.

God does realistic things which are far more astounding than any work of fiction. You can't make up things more amazing than what God does in history, nature and in our own hearts. That is where the action is.

Fleeing reality, seeking escape in magic, fiction and fantasy misdirects our attention and care, causing us to miss out on our share of the story of Life. The train leaves the station without us.

Those of us who seek reality board a train bound for the glorious fullness of God's restored rule on earth.

Day 25

Magic and fiction are wildly popular and profitable forms of studied willful ignorance. They produce unreliable maps that lead straight into mirages. Magic, fiction, fantasy, and dreams have no solid basis in facts and logic, often mixing truths, falsehoods and half-truths and glaring omissions to please the crowd.

Magic, fiction, and fantasy are based on our wishes and fears. Acting out and acting upon our dreams is basically sleepwalking. When we act upon a dream in the real world hoping for a dreamy response we are in for a shock. Unfortunately, the real world does not get the memo ahead of time and reacts to our actions out of its own needs, not to fulfill our wishes or to calm our fears.

Wishful thinking helps nothing and no one. It only wastes time, attention, and effort. The only change magic, fiction, fantasy, and dreams can yield is to increase the social status and wealth of those who peddle them as solutions to or escape from our problems. In the meantime, everything else gets worse as the real work of justice goes undone.

Day 26

God changes our minds until we learn to seek effective contact with reality. To do so, we first learn to understand why things happen the way they do, rather than wasting time and energy demanding that things happen differently so we can feel better quickly with no effort.

Contact with God is not a pacifier. God has no intention of keeping us as babies forever. God does not want us to remain children, God wants us to grow into fully functioning, competent adults and works in and around us to make us so.

God changes our hearts until we want to work realistically, not expecting things to change fast without struggle. No such change exists in nature.

Where there is quick and seemingly effortless change in nature it is where the groundwork has already been laid.

Day 27

When God makes us reality-based it does not make us depressed and dreary. It makes us happy. The root of the word "happy" is "hap," which means "luck." Before we learn how God does change, we think luck is when life is going *our* way, fulfilling our wishes and dreams.

Once we start participating in how God does change on God's terms, we realize we are finally going *life's* way! We can feel ourselves carried along in a mighty river headed to a good place. We feel lucky, which makes us feel happy, as each day is a new unfolding of a true adventure.

To go life's way is to be moving, not stagnant. To go life's way is to be moving closer to God's rule in everything we do.

Just as the fragrance of a flower grows stronger the closer we get to it; the rule of God is sweeter the more of it we integrate into our lives. The more God's way of doing things pervades every area of our lives, the more we naturally take on and give off the peace, the radiance, the fragrance of God's presence.

Day 28

God moves us away from fixing things that just break again. That is a big change and at first we don't know what to do with ourselves. But then God moves us toward creating things that naturally keep fixing and replacing themselves, as does every living system in nature.

We feel we are doing things God's way; we are going God's way; we are doing the things God does. There is something larger and wiser involved than has ever been there before.

We see results we have never seen before. They are not initially large, but what they lack in size they make up for in quality. They function at such a higher level they promise better outcomes than what we used to do, given enough time.

Our happiness grows along with a sense of anticipation and awe. Our confidence grows along with our admiration. We learn from our own direct experience that God is sovereign and has things well in hand.

Day 29

God is not the fixer. God is the Creator. The way God addresses a broken human invention that keeps breaking is to leave it behind and let it fall apart.

God replaces what does not work with something new, different, and far better than we could ever have imagined.

It is the way of Life.

It is not the way humans run museums, but then God is not a curator, endlessly preserving a frozen, highly edited past.

Day 30

If we want to know how God does change we must show up at the job site, since change is about work.

If we don't show up at all because we are off chasing a fantasy, we won't experience how God does change.

If we show up, but at a job site God has long since abandoned we won't experience how God does change.

If we show up at a job site where people are building something God would never build, we won't experience how God does change.

If we show up at a job site where people are working to preserve something God would never preserve, we won't experience how God does change.

Day 31

God won't build, improve, or preserve any kind of dictatorship, whether of a person or a class of people.

God won't build anything that gives total reign to anyone's selfishness, or to everyone's selfishness.

God only builds, sustains, and protects systems characterized by high diversity and high cooperation.

God creates forms of living organization that produce and protect justice for all of life.

That kind of organization starts in the solitude of your own heart. It starts with what must change in your attitudes, values, and behaviors for you to be an agent of justice when in contact with another of God's creatures.

Learn first how God does Happiness in your own life before learning how God does Change. We must crawl before we walk and walk before we run.

Day 32

To walk, we push against the ground, the earth. The earth pushes back against us with equal force. You might think these two forces would cancel each other and you would not move, but you do. Why? Because they act on different objects and have a vast difference in mass.

You move from where you were to a different place because you have less mass than the earth. The earth receives the force you apply to it, but it is so much more massive than you, that your effect on it is imperceptible.

On the other hand, since you are smaller than the earth, when you apply force in one direction you are moved in the opposite direction by the equal, opposing force of the earth, because you are the more movable object.

God's change follows the same laws, moving us away from one way of living toward another, completely different way of living.

As God set up the universe, to go somewhere we must leave something behind. God goes with those who leave.

Day 33

There are those who teach that good and evil are equally matched and always end up cancelling each other out. That is a myopic illusion. If we focus in too narrowly, taking into consideration only the amount of force each brings to bear at the moment of impact, and for the foreseeable future, it looks like good can't do much more than equal evil for a brief period of time, only to be defeated again later on. But we would not be factoring in the amount of mass each one has, nor the vast time scales that exist behind every masterpiece of nature.

If a golfer hits a normal golf ball, the ball will go flying because it has less mass than the combination of the golfer and golf club. Imagine a 200-pound golfer striking a nine-foot grand piano with all his might. The piano may be defaced but it will not budge. The club will bend; the handle may snap off, and the golfer may even break his wrist. Why? Because while the forces are indeed equal between what the golfer gives to and gets back from the piano, the golfer is smaller and weaker. He will suffer more harm.

It works the same way in the interaction between good and evil forces on earth.

Day 34

Evil is the function of quickly taking away what is there to take, usually the wonderful abundance that Good put in place slowly over many years. It is a terrible blow to any living system.

Human evil is part of human civilization. Add up the total weight of all humans and everything they have ever produced and compare it to the total weight of the earth and all it has ever produced. Which one has more mass? Which one has more momentum? Momentum is mass in motion.

How long has human civilization been mastering how to exploit and destroy the earth? Somewhere between ten and twenty thousand years. How long has Life been mastering how to recover, rebound, restore, replace, and create something new and better? Several billion years.

There is no comparison between the amount of momentum stored up in Life's cumulative processes and the amount stored up in human civilization. Like hitting the piano, when humans strike Life, it responds with equal and opposite force against them over time.

Humans don't have the resources to sustain the injuries from the returning blows of Life. Humans will run out of energy, then die out. Life will not. Which side do you want to be on?

Day 35

Humanity is at war with Life on earth, inflicting blow after blow. Earth is responding with blows of its own, more than civilization can sustain when the blows fall at the same time, in rapid succession.

In this war, human civilization will grow ever weaker as the earth recovers and grows ever stronger. If Evil is the ability to take away and destroy, Good is the ability to recover and build back stronger with new and better living combinations. Just as in our immune system, the next version of human civilization will have the ability to defeat what sickened the last version. In this way Good cannot do anything but win, in time.

It is simply a law of nature that Good is stronger than Evil and will prevail.

Don't let anyone tell you otherwise.

They are selling you despair so they can sell you something to relieve the pain of despair. Their product usually comes in the form of bad technology, bad religion, bad economics, bad politics combined with mood altering, addictive methods to escape the bad reality all these create. You pay with your life for what they offer.

Despair peddlers are simply clever parasites – just another form of doomed Evil.

Day 36

In God's design, Life creates, passes on, and protects the seed of the new. That seed has what it takes to survive the collapse of the old. What it has onboard is enough and no more.

What can survive, what is enough, and how that happens is precisely what God will use to repair the damage Evil has done and build something able to throw Evil off the next time.

It is easy to overlook and underestimate the power of a seed. A mighty sequoia can grow to be thirty stories tall and live more than three thousand years, yet its seed is small, drab and about the size of a pinhead.

Seeds don't attract attention; they blend into the background because it is not in the tree's interest for all its seeds to become food. Seeds don't seem to do much, and indeed for some time, they don't. Yet in them lies the future.

Seeds contain an embryonic plant, the genetic blueprints for a large complex living system of systems. The blueprints include information on how to overcome what sickened and killed its predecessors. Seeds also carry enough fuel on board to stay alive until the day of germination. Some can even remain viable for a hundred years.

Day 37

The biggest change that can happen in a life is a change in identity. We become what we identify with. Our sense of identity is to us what the internal blueprint is to the seed. What do you identify with? Who or what do you think and talk about all the time? What do you love most? What do you consider yourself to be a part of? What are you contributing to? What are you relying on? What do you love? What do you belong to? That is your internal blueprint.

Did it come from God? Do you know for sure? Is what you love and trust most connected to what has the greatest mass and momentum or is it doomed to fall apart in time?

Do you want to spend your life climbing a ladder, only to find it placed against a building that will catch fire and collapse?

Do you want to dance and party on a balcony four stories up destined to give way and go crashing down to the street, taking all your friends, your plans, and your dreams with it?

If you have never been very enthusiastic about the ladder or the party, there is a reason. The better part of you knows better. Follow that quiet voice inside and walk away. The future belongs to those who leave. Leaders are those who leave first, go the farthest into the unknown, and leave a trace others can follow.

Day 38

To love is to include in your sense of well-being whatever or whoever it is that you love. If what you love is falling apart, so is your world. If who you love is suffering, so are you. That doesn't mean you should love no one and nothing to avoid suffering. That means you should love who and what is worth loving, worth suffering over. Love what God loves, and you will be met in any suffering your love requires. You will know God with an intimacy that humans experience in no other way. Suffering is the pull of a bond. The bond either grows stronger or breaks.

If I identify most with what has less mass and momentum, because of the bond I share with it, as it goes down, so do I. It is best to let that bond weaken and perforate, so when a dying human structure breaks off and crashes to the ground, it doesn't take your entire self with it.

If I identify most with what has the most mass and momentum, because of the bond I share with it, as it goes up and onward, so do I. It is best to give that bond whatever it needs to strengthen and hold.

Day 39

God changes us until we identify with God's priorities and requirements above all other concerns. We release and leave behind anything that is doomed. We hold tight to and follow what is blessed by the daily presence of God.

What is doomed is anything God is not building or protecting. God is not building or protecting any human endeavor that is unjust today, always was and always will be.

Any human endeavor that hides it crimes against its own members to protect its reputation, so it can keep attracting new members to exploit, is an institution opposed to God and condemned by God.

What is blessed by God's active presence is any human endeavor that pursues justice as its first priority every day, entities that deal decisively with unethical behavior the minute it shows up, no matter who did it.

Day 40

God builds and protects justice for all of life on earth. That will never change. Everything else will. We bond deeply to what will never change – God's presence and character. We hold lightly or simply bypass everything else. It is only rational to do so.

We certainly don't treat as divine what is slowly falling apart and harming life along the way. Nor do we make excuses for organizations that harm the innocent, we simply abandon them. We move on with God. We take up work given to us by God and trust God to fit us to that work.

Day 41

When God gives us a work to do it will be guided and corrected by God when we must make a decision in an ambiguous situation. Since we can't predict the future, we can't be sure how things will turn out. We don't push forward with our notions. We seek God's mind and are met.

The solution is not a repeat; it is fresh and new. Like a river, always in flux, such an ongoing creative work moves continually toward God's goal for creation.

Day 42

When a work is dreamed up by unregenerate humans it will not be guided and corrected by an Infinite Mind at every point of ambiguity. Instead, at the fork in the road, unguided by God, human creations always take the wrong turn. The wrong turns always lead to catastrophe.

So yes, it is true that godless works cancel each other out in time, because they do indeed share the same mass. But we are not talking about godless works.

Move into work given and guided by God and you get off the wheel of fortune, the endless cycle of false hope and soul-crushing despair. It is the biggest change you will ever experience – to go God's way, which is Life's way, into the future.

It is the only way to be happy for long, as individuals and as a species.

Day 43

As you move into the future with God you will not have much if any company. There will not be fame or fortune. But you will participate in creation itself.

Creation has a direction and a goal. As it unfolds in and around your life you will know a fulfillment that is beyond your imagination because it is not a version of anyone else's happiness, it fits who God created you to become and your situation, not to your imagination's fantasies.

You will know a healing as deep as your wounds, for only God knows where your wounds are, how deep they are, and what it will take to touch them and turn them into something useful to Life.

Day 44

God's change does not begin with dreams or have anything to do with dreams. In fact, dreams and dreaming is where God's change work stops, because dreams hijack growth to serve human civilization as it is.

We typically get our dreams from wanting to have what others have and do what others have done, but why would we want our lives to be a copy? God creates originals.

Day 45

God does not change what exists to make it work better. A nicer thief is still a thief. A more efficient murderer is just a mass murderer. A godless civilization that wastes less of one resource will just waste something else.

Instead, God changes *out* what exists by removing what will never create justice. There are human inventions no one can modify enough to be just because from the very beginning someone conceived the invention to allow a few people to hoard more, faster. The assumption was that happiness comes from having more than we will ever need long before we will ever need it. That is a lie and nowhere in nature does God distribute resources that way for any species.

God will remove from earth systems that disrupt how God distributes resources freely, constantly, and widely - because such systems are Evil.

God replaces what God removes with something designed from the beginning to further God's purposes for earth. It will be something qualitatively, functionally different than what God removed.

Day 46

God removes unjust things in such a way that they don't come back. God takes them out by the roots. Dreams and traditions form the roots of much injustice on earth.

God removes them because they function to replace God in our hearts and minds. Both make us unavailable. Both seize and control our attention, time, devotion, willpower, and learning.

Dreams claim the future will be more securely good than ever turn out to be the case.

Tradition claims the past was more certainly good than was in fact the case.

Both provide an excuse to harm innocent lives who get in the way of getting what the dreamer wants or keeping what the tradition controls. Both can easily ignore the situation as it is and cause us to see what we want to see and not see what we don't want to see, especially in the behavior of our own group.

Day 47

It would be impossible to defend either utopian dreams or ancient traditions in court based on the evidence. Neither have been innocent in the history of human civilization.

There is a pattern: The winners, who want to hold on to their winnings, worship tradition and promote old institutions they control.

The losers or have-nots want to get what the winners have, so they worship utopian dreams and promote revolutions and movements they control.

Both take the place of God. God's change does not have its origin in dreams or traditions. God's change has its origin in God's omniscience. Only God knows what really happened in the past. Only God knows what will happen in the future. Only God knows what is best to do today, given all the forces from the past that are in play. Only God knows all the unforeseen events in the future that will impact all dreams and schemes.

Day 48

It was the Greeks who made our visual sense dominant over all the others. They created grand and intoxicating visions and carved them in stone. The Romans spread the Greek love of visual beauty over their vast empire. It didn't work out very well for either civilization. Why?

Sight is the easiest sense to fool. Dreams and traditions make extensive use of visual representations to make themselves feel real and present. It is an optical illusion.

When we arrive at our dream location we find things very different than we thought they would be – and not in a good way.

When we do historical research into how our ancestors behaved we find things that are disturbingly different than what we were told about them.

If we honestly examine the history of utopian or nostalgic movements God will use the ugly facts we find to shake our worldview to the core.

If we won't face the truth about the past we won't face the truth about the present and future. If we will face the truth about the past we are ready to face today and tomorrow by God's side.

Day 49

God initiates and guides endeavors differently. That is how God does change differently. The beginning is different. Rather than giving a famous anointed person's visions of future bliss or past glory, God uses our own sense of sight right now, right here where we are. God distributes true vision as widely as oxygen. We must just learn to use it.

God gives us opportunities to observe how thriving systems work, quietly and patiently in nature, so we can internalize the patterns of true well-being that reveal themselves over time. It allows us to sense when something is off, later when working on any human solution. Sensing something doesn't add up, we stop and ask for help.

The way God does change, sight deployed over timed serves an orienting, groundwork building function. Into a prepared, fertile mind, God plants the seed of guidance known as a calling. This seed will grow and lead to significant, lasting changes in our lives and in the lives of those we encounter.

That guiding seed of a calling grows to become dominant over what we can see right now. In fact, it must be dominant because there will be periods of time when everything we can see is so overwhelming and discouraging we will want to give up on the work of justice God called us to do.

Day 50

God's seed of initiating guidance is composed of a touch, accompanied by a quiet, gentle voice. There will be nothing hateful, cunning, unethical, self-aggrandizing or group-aggrandizing in it.

After nature has set the standard of goodness, after we have felt the touch of God's loving hand and kind wisdom in God's whisper, dreams and traditions feel silly and hollow by comparison. It will be like comparing a museum or theme park to a mountain forest or a remote, untouched beach. The air is also fresh and fragrant, our noses confirm what God promised earlier in a whisper. There is simply no comparison.

God's touch and voice resets our tastes and preferences.

That reset lasts a lifetime and turns out to be amazingly accurate. What we sensed would be there is there and more wonderful than we could have envisioned. Wonderful no longer must mean easy and comfortable. Our definition of wonderful can include problem-solving, work, setbacks, and struggle, as these serve to make the eventual breakthroughs even sweeter.

Day 51

A strong, innate, natural desire for something that exists everywhere in nature, something necessary for life to go on and flourish is no dream. It is an instinctive drive. It is well-grounded in facts and logic. If nature uses it constantly, everywhere, it is probably a pretty good thing.

Longing to have a mate and children is a good example.

We have those natural drives for a reason. God gave them to us. But since we are not omniscient we don't run off and do whatever we want to turn those desires into reality.

Instead, we bring them to God and express our longing for these natural enrichments of life. We trust God to meet and guide us regarding these desires, so we can act on them in a kind and ethical way. It is not true that "all is fair in love and war." Few things have caused more useless suffering than that pernicious idea.

We do not turn our natural God-given desires into gods because they are creations, not the Creator. Worshiping them would cause us to behave in ways that eventually harm the very things we desire. God ties desire to justice, never to envy.

Day 52

A calling is very different from a dream. Reality can crush a dream, leaving us hollowed out, adrift and imbittered.

In contrast, a calling requires reality in all its harshness to forge itself into a natural and creative force in history, serving the purposes of God.

The more adversity and the more reality a calling encounters, the stronger and more suited to the changing situation it becomes in a godly life.

The difference is the source. Dreams come from the culture around us. Callings come from the Caller.

The active ingredient in many dreams is envy. The active ingredient in callings is gratitude.

One person's dream will often collide head-on with another person's dream, harming both. One nation's dream can be another nation's nightmare.

Callings lead to peace, not endless conflict.

Day 53

God's change starts with facts and logic, not pleasant wishes. God changes a current reality by moving us effectively into it. The current reality is the only starting point there is. The current reality works the way it does for a reason, usually for many reasons. It is a real, observable, measurable combination of causes and effects which have enormous mass and a long history.

Wishing has no effect on these combinations of cause and effect as they simply lack the mass. To know God's change, we must get off the wishing track and get on another one going in a different direction for different reasons.

Only radically new values, attitudes, and disciplines have any chance of changing things for the better. This combination usually requires years to build up enough mass to have any effect.

The effect is one of exquisitely timed precision. Like a key in a lock, like a pollinator with a flower, God fits us to do just enough of the right thing, at the right time, in the right place, for the right reason, for the right amount of time, and no longer.

Massive, top-down, one-size-fits-all solutions cannot fulfill this function.

Day 54

As humans, the way we have approached our persistent problems has been the source of our persistent problems.

Our cure for the illness has been the cause of the illness, and apart from God, we don't have another cure.

Exhausted and bewildered, we finally come empty handed to the threshold of God's presence. We have unlearned our smug certainty. We come to our Creator in a neutral and open state of mind, ready for living contact with a mind far greater than ours.

We make ourselves available to learn from God, alone, in silence, on The Great Healer's schedule, for as long as it takes.

We are no longer in charge of our own development and don't want to be.

Day 55

To know how God does change we first change the way we approach our problems:

From wishing for a different reality to keenly observing the one God gave us.

From willfulness to willingness.

From resisting to assisting.

From hoarding to helping.

From talking to listening.

From fixing old things to creating new things that fix themselves.

From packaged, repetitive, crowded experiences to personal engagement in unique experiences.

When with our active participation God has made these changes in us, we begin to leave the rickety shack of human civilization and join the awesome mass and momentum of creation. Our lives are caught up in the movement of Life going wherever God is taking it, day by day.

Day 56

Inevitably events will temporarily blow us off course. We will stumble and fall over. We suffer injuries and need time to recover. We will leave cherished things along the road and never recover them. But nothing and no one will move us more than God. God is the Prime Mover.

We will not be hallucinating, mindless pawns in the games other people play. Rather, we will be receptive, responsive movers.

Day 57

God changes the structure of our minds and lives until we naturally and continually adjust to our changing environment. Until God is the one changing us we grow ever more rigid and demand an environment adjusted to us, no matter what the cost to other lives.

Adults get on with it and adjust to their situation. Children throw tantrums and demand an easier, more pleasant situation that requires no adjustment. God changes us from children to adults.

Yes, there are responsibilities attached to adulthood but there are also wonderful discoveries, made possible only by the disciplines of maturity. God changes our tastes until we prefer the wonders of responsible adulthood over the pleasures of lazy childishness or self-absorbed adolescence.

God changes what we want most. That change changes everything else.

Day 58

There is no question we must depend on resources we did not create. We need air and cannot survive without it, but we don't create air. The question is not whether we will be dependent or independent.

The question is what we will depend on and what attitude will we have toward that dependence? Forced, unnatural, unwilling dependence only builds up deep resentment. If we are healthy we seize the first opportunity to break free.

Chosen, willing, dependence on something greater and wiser than ourselves builds up a deep respect, gratitude, and anticipation. This natural state of dependence sustains us through lean times and prevents us from over consuming resources in times of abundance.

Healthy dependence draws us ever closer to the One we trust the most. There is no safer, more interesting, or more fruitful way of spending our allotted time on earth.

Day 59

God changes us from eagerly depending on things that will fail, to patiently depending on what cannot fail. We learn to embrace a willing dependence upon God to join helpful participation in God's work of creation. We don't become colorless, mindless drones in the process. Quite the opposite.

We each become unique, original, fully aware, problem-solving, choice-making, change agents right where fate placed us. Living this way, we find and fulfill our calling.

Our actions always serve the functions of justice – to increase the stock of happiness on earth for all of life.

We constantly adjust how we behave until we have a pulling-together "justice effect" on situations where there had been an "injustice effect" from a surrounding society that was pulling itself apart.

Day 60

God does not change us by *modifying* the way we depend on things or the way we treat those who depend on us.

Rather, over time, God changes *out* what we depend on and the ways we treat those who depend on us. God uses the process of repentance to *replace* harmful patterns of behavior with helpful ones, until they share a family resemblance with the pattern of interactions we see in healthy living systems elsewhere in nature.

If this sounds taxing, it is! But God gives rest along the way that truly refreshes. Then we are off again to continue the work.

Day 61

Changing from staking our happiness on one fiction to staking our lives on another fiction is a change that doesn't change anything.

It is as pointless as moving toward a new mirage instead of the mirage we last exhausted ourselves on.

Changing from chasing fictions to engaging reality? That is profound change, a change that changes the way we approach every future problem and opportunity.

Day 62

We don't run away from reality. Nor do we move against reality and attack it. Instead, we move carefully toward and then into reality with all its gritty, cause-and-effect sequences.

But now God guides us ethically. As we implement God's guidance we set in motion learning loops. We seek and use feedback from our actions. Each adjustment in our attitudes, words and actions alters the situation just enough that our next move can't be a repeat of the last one.

Guided by God, mimicking the wisdom of nature as much as we can understand it, we figure out and refine a new adjustment. As this process repeats itself, we now participate in the cycle of creation.

Changing from a life of insatiable consuming to one of useful creating is a big change.

Day 63

We act ethically in the face of any unclear situation and use the response we get to inform our next act. On each round we gain a clearer picture of the situation. There is an internal logic in what is happening. We see its real threats to justice as well as its real possibilities for a larger justice.

When it is our turn to act we choose to act on behalf of a larger justice. On God's signal, we change from being passive observers to active agents in the situation, changing it from one headed to collapse to one headed to health.

Following God's daily signal, without knowing ahead of time how it will occur, we participate in finding new, unforeseen ways to ethically address the practical challenges we face our shared the situation.

Day 64

Where others throw out the ethical imperative the minute it becomes inconvenient so they can quickly create a better solution for themselves or their group, we do the opposite.

We build in the Ethical imperative first, at the very center, no matter how inconvenient or time consuming that is. Then we work within its constraints. This creates a promising momentum others want to join.

Someone had to speak up, someone had to go first, somebody had to try something different, before something different and better could take hold. We perform that function, like the first creature in a scorching desert to find a fresh supply of water.

The less sensitive creatures, who lack the ability to find water, do have the ability to see and imitate our behaviors, setting a new thriving in motion.

Day 65

When God creates an opening in our situation, we don't wait for human permission or approval. We don't delay until we have proof it will work. It will always be a new adjustment, so we don't rely on what others did in the past to assure us we are safe to move forward.

We don't wait until others take the risk and pay the costs that come with doing something new. We don't wait until we can move on in the comfort and safety of the crowd. We don't waste time making sure there will be attention or reward for our efforts.

Our authorization to act comes from the highest source. Our comfort and strength come from the company we keep. We move along staying very close to God, never breaking contact. God's presence is the only proof we require. God then provides other proofs. Things begin to make more and more sense.

Our provisions come from the same source and always meet our needs, just in time.

Day 66

Staying close enough to God to make sure we don't lose contact with God's ethical signal is not easy or automatic. Having done it once or twice is not enough to say we have mastered how to do it.

Our imaginations can get out of hand and make fools of us. When we use wishful thinking to guide our actions we are very likely to see what we want to see and miss what is really going on. We hear what we want to hear. We don't hear that we need to hear to make good choices.

These distractions make us very vulnerable to being misled and exploited by those who appear to offer what we wish for, usually some kind of short-cut to easy, permanent happiness. We learn to recognize the beginnings of wishful thinking and to distinguish it from the touch and voice of God.

Day 67

Wishful thinking typically causes us to not see what is there. In the grip of fantasy, we overlook and deny real dangers, so we don't take measures in hand to avoid them.

Once God has changed us from being wish-based to reality-based, we more quickly sense that something is off, when something doesn't add up. We spot flattering, soothing mirages quickly and waste no energy pursuing them.

We come to the place that we just want to know what is true, not what is comforting. We can adjust to what is true, then we will be comfortable again. We cannot adjust to a hallucination, to what is not there, so there will be no lasting comfort.

Day 68

All animals have natural drives, like the need to drink fluids. The drive itself is not enough to ensure the animal's survival. It must also learn what, where and when it can safely drink, and where, when and what not to drink.

Instinct is a powerful energy source. It surges from inside a creature and is then harnessed and guided by vital information coming from the outside – the model of its parent's behavior.

There is nothing wrong with thirst. God gave us the powerful feeling of thirst to make sure we survive. God also gave us brains to observe and learn the limits within which we can safely drink. It works the same with all strong drives. They are not evil. They are essential. But undirected or misdirected they are also dangerous.

The absence of natural drives is not holiness. It is deadness. Giving in to undirected or misdirected drives is not freedom, it is madness.

God preserves our drives, then directs them into activities that help multiply the stock of happiness on earth.

Day 69

Human imagination gets its fuel from our drives. We need to feel no shame or guilt for having all our natural drives. However, our drives cannot accurately direct themselves because they can neither predict nor control the future.

As wonderful and energizing as they are, our drives are not God, so we never seek and obey them as if they are God. They are creations, not the Creator.

Passions and desires only find their true fulfillment when we place them within realistic limits, guided by an Unlimited Mind.

Under effective control, our drives will secure both our own happiness and the happiness of others, never one at the expense of the other.

Beware of religions that hold up violent conquest or violent martyrdom as the highest form of devotion to God.

God does not turn us into bullies or martyrs.

Day 70

God changes us until we willingly put all our amazing capacities, our talents, our passions, our drives, our emotions, our imaginations in service of God's purposes on earth. Only then can our faculties fulfill their purpose in our lives and in the greater story of life on earth.

Until that change happens these same mighty forces are a danger both to ourselves and to others.

How does that change happen? Through the pain of conscience.

We feel deep remorse for the lies we have believed, acted out, and passed on. We feel contrition for the things we have said and done. We hurt for the kind things we left unsaid and undone when a life placed in our path needed our touch.

Productive remorse is a defining mark of someone with a restored, healthy, growing connection to God and nature.

Day 71

Anyone who claims to have never been factually, functionally, or ethically wrong is living a lie. It is simply not possible, either for individuals or groups.

We shed cleansing tears of grief over the grief we have caused God and others. In those tears we feel a deeper intimacy with God than we knew before. God will draw us closer. We will now hear an even quieter whisper and feel an even more subtle touch.

This one change in our attitude toward our own track record sets us apart from others more than all other changes combined. It is the defining mark of a restored, living connection to God and nature.

Day 72

Our quiet time alone with God each day naturally contains some removal of the toxins we have absorbed from the culture around us. Our minds need daily cleansing no less than our blood does. Repentance does for our souls what our livers do for our blood. None of our physical or moral organs can function properly without this daily cleansing.

Remorse is proof our hearts are becoming tender and receptive again. Releasing our grip of certainty on old ways of thinking and behaving is proof we are moving closer to God. To move anywhere we must leave something behind. We release our grip and leave the errors of our culture behind.

Day 73

Holding on tight to the errors of the culture with an attitude of hardened pride, never admitting wrong-thinking or wrong-doing for fear it would signal weakness is a reliable indicator behavior.

Proud rigidity is evidence a soul is not close to God and is not moving closer. It means one has left nothing behind and is instead dragging along a mountain of lifeless baggage. Finally, the proud soul stops moving altogether, falls behind and misses out on what God has planned.

Daily repentance it the only thing that can keep us tender, sensitive, flexible, and available to God. Without this crucial practice we cannot be trusted to respond helpfully when God creates an opening for a larger justice in our situation.

Day 74

Repentance is turning away from what we were doing, then learning to do something very different. We naturally turn away from things that hurt. Repentance is feeling the hurt we have been causing others by our words, deeds, attitudes, including what we were too stingy to say or do. Neglecting to be helpful is every bit as harmful as attacking.

Repentance comes from empathy. Empathy is seeing the pain of another and feeling some of it with them, then wanting it to stop for good, as soon as possible.

Day 75

When we see our behaviors toward another creature through the loving eyes of The One who created us both and realize we are contributing to pointless suffering, we can't keep doing what we have been doing. Why we were doing it makes no difference. It must stop, now.

God built us to have both sensitive steering and powerful brakes. As change agents we will need both on a regular basis.

We must figure out what lies led us to do those things. We must stop, then turn away from those lies. If we don't, someday under stress, we will reason ourselves right back into the same behaviors, justifying the harm we cause.

A powerful vehicle with no steering or brakes is a tragedy waiting to happen, not a solution.

Day 76

Unfortunately, we are often deeply attached to harmful lies. Those we love and esteem may have modeled the lie for us. A famous person we aspire to emulate may embody the lie. We can become so attached to lies they form our very identity. We can get to the point where harming others is not just what we do but being cleverly, aggressively harmful is who we are. We can become proud of the very behaviors that grieve God's heart, then we wonder that we can't feel God's presence when we want to!

Breaking attachments to culturally endorsed lies is slow and initially painful. We must endure one passing pain to remove another, much more serious and lasting pain.

Day 77

In repentance, motivated by empathy, we hand our souls over to God for profound restructuring.

Just as we wouldn't dare try to perform brain surgery on ourselves, we don't try to remove these deeply attached lies on our own. God sets to work.

We are about to become a first-hand witness to something beyond anything another human can do. Through the restructuring of our souls, our lives, from the inside out, using unforeseen events, we will learn to recognize the touch of God's gentle hand and the tone of God's quiet voice.

Day 78

God's touch and tone will somehow get us through this profound restructuring of our souls in a way no ritual or ceremony can.

Afterwards we will instantly recognize anything different or less than God's touch and tone.

We will neither accept nor advocate a false cure for what ails us individually and as a species.

Day 79

The reason we must submit our souls to the process of repentance is we have been worshiping false gods. The driving force in our worship is envy and lust. We want something other than what we have and refuse to live without it. The false god promises to get it for us.

Lusts organized into gods always end up replacing any living, warm, reciprocal contact with other living beings we could have enjoyed.

We treat others as either useful objects or annoying obstacles.

Day 80

False gods do soothe the pain of desire for a while. Their promises are alluring and delicious.

But our deepest pain never goes away for long, so we will load up on hundreds of temporary cures, trying to remember to use them in just the right way when we feel pain.

It is always too little too late. The pain remains and grows because the temporary cures only mask the real problem. It was growing in us all along.

Cure peddlers made a fortune from our pain.

Day 81

When we turn our desires into gods we end up passively gazing at a dead thing. It won't look back lovingly into our hungry eyes because it can't. These gods will not be there for us in our time of need. They cannot hear our cries of anguish. They do not rush to help. Instead, we will feel abandoned and alone in our hour of greatest need.

Worse, along the way we become just as unperceptive and unresponsive as our dead gods. When you meet a cold, callous, calculating person you have met someone who worships a dead god.

Day 82

Sometimes our dead gods have a living representative. This person lives large and performs on a large stage.

If we get the chance to go backstage to meet the high priest of our dead god, we discover it is all an act. The contrast between the person's public persona and private behavior is shocking. There is no connection between what they say and what they do.

Once we come to worship only the Creator we have a completely different experience from adoring a human celebrity.

Day 83

The process of repentance pulls back the curtain to see how God does things, including change. As we go backstage we find that what God directs us to do consistently is what other long-lived social species also do consistently.

We also find what God directs us avoid doing other long-lived social species also avoid doing.

God is not a phony. Rather than feeling shocked and shaken when we observe firsthand how God does things, we feel awe in the presence of the infinite wisdom of our Creator.

It is hard to settle for anything less after that. We want to see that same wisdom embodied in our own lives, in our own work, starting with the smallest things we do.

Day 84

What real repentance does is bring real intimacy with God into the very center of our lives. Real repentance is intimate, direct contact, conducted in solitude. Sometimes there are tears as we feel the pain we have caused God and others. The tears mean we are not dead inside yet.

There can be tears of relief, as we sense we have finally brought our burdened conscience to the one place where the hurtful patterns of behavior can eventually be broken off and replaced.

Day 85

Human institutions often set up systems of cheap, false repentance.

What false repentance does is put us in the presence of another human, or a group of humans in public. There may be tears, but some of them are for show. False repentance has the same effect as no repentance. Both increase the distance between us and God, but false repentance is worse because it uses God's name and ethical requirements as props in a show, without taking either seriously.

None of us behave the same way when we know another human is watching, much less when we know a crowd is watching. We don't pray in front of others for this reason. No one can resist the temptation to gain quick social points by appearing pious.

Day 86

Real repentance directly addresses our real, authentic, unstaged behaviors. Real repentance deals with who we really are, not who we want others to think we are. It exposes and confronts anything we admire and trust more than God. Real repentance dislodges and flushes out patterns we have accepted as normal but appear nowhere in nature.

Real repentance will expose behavior that is deceitful, designed to mislead and take advantage of others.

Real repentance will expose behaviors that are conceited, when we mislead ourselves to hold an unrealistic opinion of ourselves or our group, one our track record cannot support. Everyone knows it is a fantasy except us.

Real repentance replaces habits that harm others with habits that help others.

Real repentance replaces habits that sever us from reality, the habits that make us useless to others and harmful to ourselves.

Day 87

God alone knows exactly where all the culture's lies have taken rooted in our souls, and where they came from in the first place. We often don't remember how they came into our lives, but they are now tucked away in the secret folds of our brains and connected to cherished memories and strong emotions.

God brings cleansing, clarifying light into dark places daily, starting with the backlog of habits that built up over years.

Day 88

One of the habits that most separates us from God is the habit of mistaking a contrived image for reality. There is something about looking at an alluring image of something instead of something real that flicks our brains into sleep mode. Under the spell of imagery, we start living inside a dream. If millions look at the same image millions dream the same dream at once.

The minute we go into dream-sleep mode we disconnect from our real, current situation and all its messy, inconvenient details. The minute we disconnect from reality, we stop adapting to it. The minute we stop adapting to reality we drop out of the school of life on earth. The minute we drop out, we start to degrade.

When we drop out of life we lose one adaptive ability, then another, because we have no need for them.

Day 89

We know God is now rescuing and repairing us once we can tell what is really serious and what is not. Losing a capacity essential for long-term survival is as serious as it gets.

In nature, when we don't use something, we lose it. There is not enough energy to do everything our brains need to do, so the brain redirects energy from what we aren't using to what we are using.

What we do repeatedly grows, what we stop doing with any frequency, shrinks. If we stop connecting to reality through observation and reason, we lose the ability to connect with reality and adapt to it.

Adapting is largely a function of self-correction, leaving behind errors, things that no longer work in our situation.

Serious errors are the behaviors that harm what we and those we love will need to face together the challenges none of us can face alone.

Day 90

By not using our natural error-correcting capacities regularly, it is possible to lose so many that we pass the point of no return. For example, a body with a serious auto-immune disease can lose the only thing that can cure any disease, including the auto-immune disease itself. Painful decline and death lie around the corner.

We have a social auto-immune disease and are nearing the point of no return when we no longer feel empathy for the suffering of others. It is at an acute stage when we feel no remorse for anything we did individually or collectively that contributed to others' suffering.

Losing empathy for others is a problem that prevents the solving of all other problems. It is the first stage of failure of a social species.

There is nothing more serious.

Day 91

We are caught in a deadly down draft once we are both unable and unwilling to seek and accept having our ideas, values, attitudes, and behaviors corrected directly by God daily.

If what we have been part of is godless and harms life, we must get out while we can still cry.

If we can still cry, we can still cry out – to God. God alone can hear our cry and pull us out of a deadly down draft before it is too late.

Day 92

The more adaptive abilities we lose the more frightening reality becomes because we can't cope and we know it. The more frightening we find reality the more we flee into an impenetrable, invulnerable world of contrived images, theories, and dreams.

Nothing makes us more vulnerable than pursuing a state of invulnerability found nowhere in nature.

Pursuing and hording unnatural invulnerability sets in motion a vicious cycle in which weakness leads to more weakness. There is a specific point at which the vicious cycle can be broken. First, God breaks the habit of fleeing from life. Only then can any further change-work be done.

Day 93

Just as a child must first learn to read before she can learn about anything else, we must first learn to read reality instead of fantasy. To learn to read reality we learn first to direct our attention away from any imagery created by humans. A symbol of the ocean is no substitute for the ocean. A word for a thing is not the thing itself.

Symbols, imagery, and words can serve a useful temporary purpose as a placeholder, but they easily overstay their welcome. What stands alongside something real that is easier and quicker to grasp than the real thing can quickly become a substitute for the real thing.

If we think by saying or singing "be kind" we have now actually been kind, we are deluding ourselves. We must experience the reality that kind behavior can be costly and inconvenient and still practice kindness before we can think of ourselves as kind people. Otherwise, we're fooling ourselves, but no one else.

The imagery humans have contrived is dead. We can't afford to treat it as if it is alive. It makes no difference whether ancestors or contemporaries created the imagery. Humans are not God no matter what century they inhabit.

Day 94

A good rule of thumb: if an animal won't stop and look at something for a long time, it is unwise to look at it for a long time hoping to find divine meaning and direction.

Animals know what is alive and what is not. What is alive and real can be touched, felt, and smelled. A living thing registers an animal's presence and responds immediately to what the animal does. What is not actually present in the room does nothing, or if it is something automated it just keeps doing what it was doing as if the animal is not there.

Animals are still connected to life on earth. Animals don't become entranced by imagery, but unfortunately humans do.

Always ask, "if I trust this imagery and do what its creators ask me to do, who benefits immediately, in material terms, for sure?"

If it is human institution, something is off.

If it is another specific life you know and share a space with right now, it is a reliable signal, functioning like a sign with a symbol of the ocean pointing to the ocean.

If the symbol makes no claim to be the reality itself and asks for no contribution, it was probably funded and left by those who have gone before, those who want you to arrive safely at the reality that is beyond all symbolism.

Day 95

Once the trance of false imagery is broken, we learn to direct our attention away from imagery and toward God, who is and always will be invisible. God helps us direct our newly released attention to the nature we find around us, then to real people in our lives.

A new virtuous cycle has begun. Strengths create more strengths as our powers of observation and adaptation come back online and grow stronger the more we use them.

We see more of reality sooner and adapt to it sooner and more effectively, which opens our eyes to more reality to see and adapt to. The cycle continues.

We have re-entered the river of life itself with all its force, its twists and turns.

Day 96

As we move along in the river of life, one dream after another evaporates which God replaces with a newly-discovered reality, then another - until we hit something that will not budge.

It is some kind of log jam. A log jam is locked and rigid, allowing nothing to move. It clogs up the river, which otherwise would be unlocked and fluid, bringing life to everything it touches.

Irresistible force has met immovable object. Something must give way.

Day 97

In a log jam there is a key log. Loggers used to float logs down rivers to get them to the sawmill. Sometimes the logs would jam up, usually at a bend in the river, allowing no more logs passage.

Adding more logs would only add more mass and weight, making the log jam even tighter.

Instead of doing more of what they had been doing, the loggers stopped and did something else. One of them had earned the reputation as the "key logger."

The keylogger would study the log jam, often for days, from a high vantage point overlooking the river and the log jam. It was rarely obvious which log was the culprit.

Finally, the key logger identified which log held all the others in place and directed crews below to place a charge of dynamite on it to blow it up. Once the key log shattered into pieces, all the other logs started to move. Now the same forces that once locked the jam in place make everything move through with increasing speed.

Removing the key log released pent up energy and put it to work.

In our souls, the key log is the lie that holds a cluster of other lies in place. The key log is something bad and unnecessary that we have come to believe is good and necessary. The key log also prevents the entry into our lives of something we have come to believe is bad and unnecessary that is in reality good and necessary if we are to participate in life on earth on God's terms.

Day 98

God is our key logger.

Repentance will lead us on occasion to the removal of a huge lie, a notion that was never true, but we built our lives around it anyway. This big lie has commanded our respect and loyalty for years and most everyone around us venerates it without question.

Big lies are often national, tribal, or religious in nature. They are usually ancient. Big lies give permission to moral, economic, and political insanity. Humans build big fortunes and reputations by keeping big lies alive and powerful enough to control and exploit millions of other lives.

The big lie is the main thing that blocks us from ever knowing God intimately and experiencing first-hand how God does change. It is also what causes our own lives to block contact with God for others. The big lie is the reason what we do contradicts what we say we value.

Day 99

The big lie is an insult to God because it claims to do a better job of meeting our needs than God. Either the lie goes away, or God stays away. Something must give. It is our choice.

Abandoning the big lie is scary as it sets us adrift in a now unfamiliar world we have lost the capacity to deal with, the world of ever-changing reality. But trying to live inside any lie, over time, is far worse. The bigger the lie the worse it gets.

The closer we examine the big lie, the less evidence we find to support it and the more evidence we find that refutes it.

Day 100

Set against the big lie is The Big Truth: Life is the constant process by which new and different components combine in new and different ways. Life causes increasing complexity to work toward a new, unforeseen function known only to God, the author of Life. The closer we examine The Big Truth the more evidence we find to support it, and we find no evidence that refutes it.

At some point it gets personal. Will I reject any new higher complexity, or will I help it along?

It is the most important choice I will ever make. I must make the choice anew each day as I encounter another version of the big lie, vying for my attention and trust.

Day 101

If I reject a new, higher complexity as it starts to emerge I am attempting to stop the flow of Life, to dam up the river. I will need a key log, a popular lie that gives me the crowd's permission to stand in the way of Life and say "stop!"

There will always be big lies available for sale and lots of people who buy them. Like getting drunk, all I need to do is choose my preferred drink and guzzle it down. No critical thinking, no separating fact from fantasy. Just let the soothing intoxication flow in to take over and alter my mood. The change in mood will be easy, fast, and pleasurable. Soon it will take over and alter my life, becoming the way I approach every problem and opportunity.

Every day I am free to choose whether I help or hinder Life, but I am not free to choose the consequences of my choice. In God's justice, the consequences of our choices are built into the choices themselves.

Day 102

We choose differently. Once we realize Life is creating a new, higher complexity we decide to help it along, no matter what that requires from us. We devote our lives to that purpose. We devote the best God has given us to advance the best God wants to happen on earth. It is the most noble thing we can do with the freedom God gave us.

Devotion to one thing requires rejecting other things so I can concentrate my powers on one goal, the highest one.

Day 103

As an act of devotion...

We choose not to turn off our brains; we turn our brains on. We choose not to ignore facts. We gather facts and organize them.

We choose not to live inside entertaining fantasies. We seek verifiable and measurable observations of reality.

We choose not to embrace illogical nonsense and magical thinking. We like the rigor of logic and get better at using it.

We know things don't just happen. There are reasons things happen, especially if they happen repeatedly. We like figuring out the reasons why things happen, and other things don't.

Day 104

We don't close down our lives to fit our current coping mechanisms, leaving us feeling smug, superior, and comfortable.

We open up our lives.

We expand our coping mechanisms to care for the lives around us, so we can remain truly alive and helpful.

Day 105

This daily struggle to expand our capacities leaves us humbled by the difficulty of the work and concerned about our own competence to do it.

But we know God is our teacher and trainer. There is no better developmental process available.

We know God is not cruel. God does not set us up to fail. We stay close to God and constantly seek direction and correction when we know we don't know for sure what is the best thing to do next.

We find we have become good enough at the work to meet the needs God calls us to meet, in 24-hour increments.

Day 106

As our capacity for problem-solving grows, we invite in more information about the messy, confusing, changing complexity in our situation, including its mysteries and contradictions.

These things don't scare God. We don't try to protect God, or our belief in God from the impact of new facts. We are not children.

We want to understand why things are the way they are. We go beneath the surface because that is where God meets us. That is where we find the beginnings of new and better solutions.

Day 107

There are also natural consequences for making the choice to help with the unfolding complexity God is bringing about. Everything in our lives initially becomes harder, but over time it also becomes more natural and less contrived. Our lives simplify, requiring much less maintenance.

One of the first consequences of clearing the log jam in our souls is that we sleep better than we used to and wake up refreshed. We feel less alone. We are gripped by less anxiety. We worry less.

There are many more natural consequences of devotion to God's way, each providing us with more to work with to help nature along.

Day 108

Our defining life choice is to expand our understanding and competence to cope with complexity so we can keep pace with what Life is doing. To "attend" means to show up, to deal with, and to stretch.

Repentance is the constant process of stretching our ability to recognize, honor and support the increasing diversity and complexity of Life. It is relearning to use our attention for its intended purpose.

To repent daily is to embrace the Big Truth, to embrace the reality of why God created our species. The Big Truth helps life and keeps us on the same path as life.

Things get really interesting the farther we get from our old log jam. We wouldn't go back if we could!

Day 109

God often uses unforeseen, shocking external events to dislodge a big lie stuck right in the center of our lives. The shocks bring big, permanent losses. The losses force us to realize we have been lied to all along. It was all a mirage. It feels cruel, but it is an act of mercy on God's part.

The shocks unblock the conduits of direct connection to our Creator, channels clogged with inherited nonsense, allowing nothing new and better to enter. God put those conduits in our brains, now God takes them back and puts them in service of justice.

We lose old false certainties, but we gain new freedoms. We gain new true certainties by unpacking verifiable reality. There is no comparison between the new certainties and the notions we held dear when we were chasing fantasies or retelling unverifiable legends and myths.

Day 110

Once our log jam clears out, we learn to work with God daily to dislodge and flush out whatever junk we picked up the day before, but there is a difference.

This daily cleansing did not take place for years. Issues piled up behind the log jam, unresolved. Until this backlog of unaddressed habits and attitudes is resolved we carry so many toxins with us that God didn't let us make deep contact with others. God kept us somewhat in quarantine lest we pass on our remaining errors through word or deed.

Finally, there comes a day when we no longer pass on toxins, and we enter each new day with the benefit of hindsight. We can put the log jam breaking, backlog clearing experience in perspective for others in a way we couldn't when we were in the messy middle of it.

God allows us to gently come alongside others who are having their own log jam removed. They are as mad and scared as we were to lose their big, organizing lie, the one they built their lives and identities around. Should they ask, we can help them understand what is happening and why it is necessary. One day they will do the same for someone else.

Day 111

After God has worked through the backlog cluster of old lies and now cleanses our minds of toxins each morning before we head out, we start to interact with others in a new way. Others interact with us doing everyday ordinary things that ordinary people do to manage their lives. The perceptive among them sense the interaction is not an everyday ordinary experience.

Something is different about us.

Without planning to, our now spontaneous, habitual behaviors display the rule of the One we trust and admire most.

Day 112

There is also something different between us.

Between two or more people who have experienced God's cleansing, correcting mercy, there is a quiet recognition.

We see it in each other's' eyes, often welling up with tears of grateful joy as we exchange stories of how God met us, changing the way we see all Life around us. In fact, for the first time we do see all Life around us and can learn from its wisdom. We can share what we discover with each other and marvel.

We share each other's burdens, which cuts them in half. We share each other's joys, which doubles them. We are there for each other in a way we weren't before. Our central concern used to be what we got out of the interaction.

Now, we know God provides all that we need, so our central concern is to be useful to God and helpful to each other.

Day 113

God's presence in our lives shows in our behavior. Especially our unplanned, reflexive, habitual and non-verbal behaviors.

There are harmful things we never do that others do; things we once did as well.

There are helpful things we consistently do that others do inconsistently, if ever. We were once inconsistently helpful as well.

There are helpful things we do far more often than others do, and more often than we used to.

Day 114

Before we lived in direct, correcting contact with God, our helpful actions were often just a tactic we used to help us get something we wanted.

We are now uncomfortable with ourselves if we're not helpful. Why? Because now helpful actions simply express who we are, whether we get something out of it or not.

We don't want to live in a world where God's values are not real, so we make them real by the choices we make. We make God's values real even if what we must do to make them real causes us to give up things the unhelpful get.

Values that only cost words are not real. Values that cost real advantages are more real than those advantages. This is how you can distinguish between those who claim to know God and those who really know God.

Those who know God use deeds with few if any words, those who don't know God use words, with few if any deeds.

Day 115

As God's presence comes to life in our behaviors, there are things we do far less often than others do, and less often than we used to. You can see God's presence is our approach to conflict. We don't go looking for conflict, but sometimes we must put up a fight.

When we must fight, we attack lies using facts and logic. We don't attack the liar, using insults and intimidation.

Day 116

There are things we now do differently than others do, and differently than we used to.

For instance, we use modern technology when it is more efficient, but we don't think we are missing out if we don't have the latest gizmos, nor do we worship those who create them.

The newest technology is just another log in the log jam, just another change that changes nothing about humanity's moral trajectory.

Technology is no substitute for God. It is not alive, no matter how life-like it may pretend to be.

Machines have none of the wisdom of Life and do nothing to further justice. As dead things, machines cannot seek and respond to guidance from God. We do not hand over our attention and energy to the control of machines of any kind for any reason for any length of time. To do so would be to participate in death.

Day 117

One of the things that changes under God's rule is how we enjoy the many wonderful pleasures of life. "Enjoy" means "a given joy,' in contrast to a grabbed and horded joy. How any pleasure comes into and out of our lives makes a big difference.

In God's economy, surprising, enjoyable, pleasant objects and experiences are provided as needed. We find them satisfying and sufficient when we need something to refresh us. God knows what we need, how much we need, when we need it, and for how long because God knows us better than we know ourselves. Like cold water stationed along the course of a marathon for the runners, refreshments exist for us, but we don't exist to consume refreshments.

We don't abandon the race and settle down next to the watering station. We don't grab all the water, so no other runners get any. We don't grab as much as we can carry in case there isn't any more coming and try to continue the race dragging along an ever-bigger pile of goodies behind us.

Since we know God will provide again when we need something, we enjoy it, set it down, leave it behind - and keep moving in service of our calling.

Day 118

The reason God entrusted humans with such unique capacities is so we could cultivate the fullest possible cooperation between the lives around us. We will need all those capacities to perform our function on earth.

We don't exist to enjoy pleasures. We exist to facilitate and protect Life's full unfolding on earth in all its wonderful, unforeseen, unplanned, ever-higher complexity and diversity. Pleasures exist to refresh us along the way as we fulfill the reason we exist.

Putting our capacities in service of any other purpose, like piling up pleasures, harms the earth, and leads to the extinction of species, including our own.

God would never guide an individual or society to do such a foolish thing. Any teaching that suggests otherwise is a lie against Life; another key log God will shatter and remove by force.

Day 119

Life direction and meaning is about what we choose to pursue and collect. For us, good things pass easily into and out of our daily lives. Good things do not provide us with our life's direction and meaning. They are simply perks of the job; refreshments stationed along our path.

We can take them or leave them. We learn to be as happy when we are prevented from getting something or somewhere as we are when we are permitted to have something or go somewhere. We know we don't know best, and we know God does.

Why do we eventually get to the point that we can quickly and gracefully release the very things we used to cling to? Because there is something invisible and higher to pursue. There are richer things to collect. If you can put a price on it is not that valuable. The most valuable things are priceless.

Day 120

We pursue insight into how God fosters cooperation between lives. We work to turn those insights into practical skills. To do this we often migrate from location to location, from role to role.

We become mobile, moving to different environments where we will find the next set of insights.

Day 121

Our gathered insights into how God fosters cooperation don't sit in a static pile. When God teaches us something we find ourselves needing to use it within days. Through trial and error, God expects us to use the challenge at hand to turn our lessons into skills. God provides a margin of error while we are learning, but not too much. It is one of the ways God shows mercy. God expects us to show the same kind of mercy while the peopled in our lives struggle to learn.

In time our new skills converge into habits fitted to meet unforeseen challenges. These habits become a kind of instinctive wisdom. Wisdom is a demonstrable skill for meeting ever changing situations as members of a social species. True wisdom naturally models how to behave to keep a living social system in a healthy, cooperative state.

Just as it does among elephants, among us leadership goes to the wisest, not the most selfish. We can safely imitate their behaviors because doing so makes everything better for everyone.

Day 122

Godless cultures praise persistence and determination in pursuit of an ever-growing static pile of personal or group privileges, then passed on those privileges to those didn't work for them.

Static, growing piles of unearned privilege passed on from generation to generation is not a recipe for justice. It is a recipe for war.

We too value persistence in the face of difficulty and adversity, but in the pursuit of justice, motivated by love.

Day 123

God has nothing to do with unearned privilege. You will never see multi-generational, unearned privilege in nature. God abhors all systems of caste, class, and race as such systems waste the talents of innocent millions by depriving them of resources and opportunity. God assesses lives on case-by-case basis, not on a case by category basis. So do we.

Any religion, philosophy, political or economic system that teaches otherwise is an abomination to God and will pay the highest price for its crimes against Life – it will cease to be hosted by earth.

If we don't learn from the book of Life, Life itself will erase us from the book of Life.

Day 124

There is rank in nature, but it works differently. In nature those with the highest rank have earned it individually and continue to earn it every day. A good example is elephants.

Among elephants, the one the group trusts to provide direction is the wisest among them, not the most aggressive. The wisest is the most experienced, aware of the changing environment, and decisive. The wisest knows how to figure out what to do next. The group follows its wise leader because she has a solid track record of making choices that materially benefited the whole group, not just herself.

The group remembers that its leader has made choices that protected the most vulnerable - the very young, the very old, the pregnant, the sick and the injured, as much as was possible for as long as was possible.

They can't guarantee it, but in nature wise leaders give every member of their group the best chance possible to make it through the most challenging times.

Day 125

In nature among social species, any member of a group will be vulnerable to harm at some point in their life, naturally, through no fault of its own. Under wise leadership, each group member learns that if it has contributed to the survival and success of the group, in its time of need it will receive the protection of the group, decreasing the odds of being seriously harmed.

Social species also punish freeloaders, those who use the benefit of the group but refuse to contribute to the group's well-being.

If these ways of behaving were not in place, any social species would have gone extinct long ago.

Social species survive together, or they don't survive at all, much less thrive.

Day 126

We find there are times when we must live migratory lives, moving from one place in need of justice to the next place in need of justice. Danger and resources do not appear in the same place and in the same form all the time.

Danger can move toward us – and we must move to get out of harm's way. Danger can envelope those we love – and we must move to stand between them and danger. When danger is on the move, it is unethical not to move in response.

Resources can move away from us – and we must move to make sure our young have what they need to become what God created them to be. When opportunity is moving away, it can be unethical not to move in response.

Day 127

If and when there is an ethical reason to move and we refuse, as God's change agents, we find we can't live happily in our settled comfort. On the other hand, if and when there is an ethical reason to stay put, we find we can't live happily if we wander off chasing thrills and adventure.

Our goal is to be useful to God and helpful to Life. If that requires moving, we move. If that requires staying, we stay.

We cannot happily live otherwise because God created and called us to serve a protective, restorative, regenerative function for life on earth.

Day 128

Our bodies do not contain enough blood to keep all our organs always functioning fully. Instead, our bodies move refreshing, energizing, healing blood around to where it is needed when it is needed.

Our bodies store up immune responses in our lymph nodes and then send them to where they are needed, when they are needed. In our bodies vital resources stay in constant motion, they do not pool up and stagnate.

God is everywhere at once. There are not enough of us to be everywhere at once. God moves us to where we are needed. Placement decisions belong to God, not us.

The process of moving itself clears out a lot of outlived junk. We sort out what we really need from what we don't ever use. We live more lightly with each successive move.

Day 129

In the history of life on earth, when the environment changes dramatically in such a way that surviving the old way is no longer possible, a sharp divide emerges. Many species go extinct, while a few survive and go on to thrive.

The mobile, cooperative, and highly adaptable generalists survive and go on to thrive in the altered environment. Generalists have many different ways of surviving. They can quickly abandon ways of surviving the environment no longer supports and start using one the environment will support, after a period of trial and error.

The settled, solitary, and rigid specialists perish. Specialists have only one way of surviving so when the supply of what they need to survive dwindles they kill each other over what remains.

Rather than increase the odds of survival, competition among them as individuals guarantees their own extinction as a group.

Day 130

God teaches us to be mobile, cooperative, and competent at many different skills.

During times of chaos and collapse, the migratory skill set becomes more important than it was in times of stability and growth.

God makes sure we are good at creating justice whether we live in a settled or migratory state. Over the course of our lives sometimes we need to settle down and sometimes we need to be migratory.

Our young need to see us model both settled and migratory ways of living so they know when, where and how to use each way of living.

They see that what makes us godly and useful to God is not being settled or migratory, it is staying receptive and responsive to God's directing ethical signal in any situation, at any phase of life.

Day 131

As we arrive at our new duty station, whether a new job in the same location or in a new neighborhood, we quietly begin to stand out to our new neighbors and co-workers. To them we are a curiosity - wonderful strangers from another dimension.

Since we have turned away from the lies of the culture and turned toward God's rule, we behave differently. That is enough. We are silent about our intimate connection with God. We let our actions and results speak for us.

Behavior communicates more honestly and accurately than words. Behavior signals what lies in the depth of our souls, who we trust, what we hold most dear and will not harm.

Deep waters are quiet, shallow waters babble constantly.

Day 132

We don't use God-talk. We don't use esoteric convoluted insider language to appear deep and profound. We don't string together coined terms that mean something only to people who go to regular meetings where everyone uses them and reads the same books.

Instead, we communicate through simple behaviors which anyone, any child, can understand.

When we do talk, we talk about things all creatures experience in common, not elite experiences that signal how much money we have.

Our behaviors don't just say something about us to other humans. For instance, out on a walk, when we encounter healthy happy dogs, they can tell Whom we have spent time with in the morning. They are happy and healthy because they feel safe and loved, so a new deeply loved and loving person feels familiar. They know we are part of earth, just as they are. We are earthlings, not worldlings.

To other creatures that know their role in creation, we feel like family, because we are.

Day 133

There are daily habits that keep us connected to God, to Earth, and to our role on earth:

The cleansing of daily repentance, removing out errors, alone with God,

seeking no one to function as a go-between with God.

patient, not looking for a gimmick to make contact with God easier and faster,

bearing the confusion and difficulty of sorting out for ourselves what is true and what is false, what is helpful and what is harmful,

holding our actions up to the standards set by nature,

seeking and responding to God's correction where we don't yet live up to those standards,

committing to behave differently the next time,

practicing the new behavior the next time the opportunity arises, knowing it will very soon.

Only these habits can accrue enough force to liberate us from the habitual grip of dead gods, long ago forced on humans through violent conquest.

Day 134

We can choose to live in a state of constant repentance and know God's presence. In God's presence alone we will come to know how God does change.

Or - we can refuse to live in a state of constant repentance and not know God's presence. If we do not know God's presence we will not know how God does change. If we still want to be change agents and "change the world," we will be sucked into the ways humans attempt to do change apart from God.

We take one step forward, one step back, two steps forward, three steps back - an exhausting tedium. Everything we do to make things better ends up making things worse. There are unforeseen events that upend our plans. There are unforeseen reactions and consequences because of our endeavors. We can't know the thoughts and intentions of others and are stunned by their acts of betrayal.

We chased an alluring mirage right into quicksand. We use our own efforts against ourselves. Repeatedly, we experience false hope followed by bitter despair. We live through the tortuous unraveling and collapse of everything we spent our lives building or defending.

We die knowing our work didn't work. We spent our lives in vain and can't get them back. Playing God comes at the highest possible cost.

Day 135

False hope typically starts with poetry, soaring oratory, and vivid imagery, artfully representing something glorious just over the horizon.

Those peddling false hope who have the deepest pockets will hire the most stunningly gifted visual and musical artists to glorify their endeavors. In every artful representation of The Ideal, the artist hides the ugly vices of humans apart from God and exaggerates the potential virtues of humans that will magically emerge "just as soon as" some change in law, custom or leadership is made. Even when the change is made, humans don't behave much better for long. It was just a cleverly marketed mirage.

Knowing an artful representation of God or some utopia or some previous golden age is to know an artful representation. It is *not* to know what is compellingly real - God and nature. Knowing propositions *about* God and nature is also not the same as knowing God and nature by direct contact.

By contrast, we discover to our delight that what is real needs no representations or living representative. What is real represents itself, if only we will draw close enough, stay there, and take the time to learn what reality has to teach.

Day 136

There are diseases like scurvy that occur when the body lacks an essential nutrient, like vitamin C. The painful cluster of symptoms indicates a critical deficiency. In societies, the multiplying of artful representations of God or replacements for God reveals there is little if any living contact with God or nature. One of the painful symptoms of living disconnected from God and nature is inability to create peaceful cooperation and mutual benefit out of diversity.

In contrast, once we have learned to stay in living contact with God, we feel no attraction to artful representations of God. Instead, we have a natural repulsion at the very thought of any human creation taking the place of God in our lives or in our community. We also naturally develop an attraction to unfolding diversity and want to protect it.

Day 137

Defending representations of God or God replacements reveals the presence of a deadly disease: the refusal to make living, direct contact with God. This disease of refusal comes from thinking that contact with God should be convenient, quick, easy, and soothing, as if The Creator is just another a consumer product.

With the refusal to make direct contact with God comes the refusal to alter one's ethical behavior. Those disconnected from God suspend God's ethical imperative the minute their personal interests are at odds with it. Worldlings can change their values as easily as they change their clothes, with astonishing speed. Their conscience does not bother them at all, because the disease has killed it.

The disease ends in extinction.

Day 138

There is something about worship canned for convenience that produces ethics canned for convenience. Canned ethics is a limited set of rules, giving permission to do anything not on the list of prohibitions. Canned ethics also prescribe a limited list of good things to do. Once those few, cheap, easy, gestures have been dutifully and solemnly performed, you can behave any way you want. Canned worship always centers around a highly stylized representation of God created by a human.

Representing God is the attempt to limit God's presence to when, where and how God can show up, as if God is a circus act we can pay to go see at our convenience. Canned ethics are a haggling ploy. The idea is to get down to the absolute minimum cost of devotion to God and get the maximum benefit from God in return.

As if the Creator of the Universe is in such a weak power position humans can coerce a deal from God! How insulting. No one teaching or believing such nonsense will know God's presence and active guidance. No society built on such a religion will escape the consequences of smearing the name of God.

Day 139

God alone represents God. God alone choses when, where and how God's presence will be felt.

God's freedom is unlimited and shows itself in constantly new, intimate, and surprising ways, at inconvenient times, in obscure places, with no audience watching. Since we don't control when God shows up no one can schedule it ahead of time. There will be no applause directed at any human's ability to conjure God's presence. God condemns magic and does not respond to magic tricks.

In history, God's presence has been felt anew, qualitatively, in the way of living found among invisible, ignored people with no social status or power, but a people who have long sought and followed God's ethical guidance no matter what the cost.

The ethical imperative is not an optional add-on for these people; it is what defines them.

Day 140

We have had 10,000 years of canned worship without the real presence of God, with only canned or optional ethics.

As a new rising people, it is our birthright to finally know the real presence of God without canned worship, without any pretense of haggling with the Creator to get a better deal.

We claim that as our birthright. It is our role on earth. With any role comes a set of guiding priorities and firm limits. We don't stop at knowing *about* the priorities and limits intellectually. Through study and practice, we come to identify with and embody God's priorities and accept God's limits in our daily behavior.

Day 141

With our birthright we accept our role. Just as a forest ranger knows things must happen and certain things must be stopped for the forest to remain healthy and productive, we too gladly accept God's priorities and limits that regulate how we interact with the part of creation entrusted to our care.

Each situation requires particular actions today to prevent harm and create health. Another forest, another day - a different set of actions, but the priority of preventing harm and cultivating health never changes.

Day 142

Anything that claims to sit alongside God, making God safer and more convenient to know, will quickly take the place of God.

Any canned, repetitive, mass-distributed, scheduled, convenient way of accessing God is a danger to life because it separates us from God's direct, immediate guidance.

Separated, we can't perform the role God designed for us.

Any quick, easy, one-size-fits-all activity that claims to rid us of our guilt, becomes a substitute for real repentance. Lacking real repentance, we continue to do harm and miss the critical moments when our help is needed. Life around us suffers as a result.

Just as there is no substitute for vitamin C, there is no substitute for direct contact with God and the daily repentance that comes with that contact. We get morally sick and so does the whole living system around us.

Day 143

No police detective would think it was a coincidence that a certain person is always in the neighborhood when a murder is committed, even if the neighborhoods are miles from each other or the murders occurred in different decades. The "coincidence" leads to the murderer.

Without fail, over the course of human history, ever grander religious rituals show up at the same time and same place as entrenched systemic social injustice.

There is a reason.

Any substitute for direct contact with God and nature gives humans room to chip away at the Ethical Imperative. We start to think since we've done our rituals we have bought off God for the week. We are free to behave how we want to get what we want. And if we do something that bothers our conscience, there is a cheap, convenient ritual to take care of that too, so there is no need to concern ourselves with the well-being of others, especially those who are different from ourselves.

The substitute for direct contact with God is deadly because it systematically kills off the conscience, especially the sense of collective responsibility for what happens to the weak in our community.

Day 144

Substitutes will always be packed and sold in some way. Substitutes can be purchased. There is almost always some kind of receipt to document the purchase. There will always be an incentive to buy in bulk – to commit to a longer time frame to get a better deal.

Ethical behavior is always about a unique, timely adjustment to the needs of another life. If I *make* an adjustment I must do the work myself. If I *purchase* the adjustment I am paying someone to do the work for me. *Making* an adjustment changes me. *Purchasing* an adjustment leaves me unchanged. I was a passive consumer before I purchased the adjustment, and I am still a passive consumer after I purchased the adjustment.

If I am unchanged I cannot bring God's change to the situation in which I find myself.

Day 145

Anytime I let someone do something vital for me I take a double loss. I lose the feeling of growing into a new competence that comes with successfully dealing with today's challenge in a new and better way.

I also lose the feeling of triumph dealing with tomorrow's challenge. The next time a similar challenge arises I still don't know what to do except to find my supplier and make another purchase.

"Helpful" merchants take from us more than they provide for us if their "help" replaces making contact with God and finding the solution to today's ethical challenge. They save us from confusion and struggle, but in so doing they weaken us to make us dependent on their products and services for life.

Day 146

It is the unique way we use resources that keeps us strong, flexible, and self-reliant. We trust God's wisdom. We don't disrupt God's distributed system that provides just enough, just in time, for all of life, everywhere.

God has already placed resources where they are needed right now. We are not allowed to send these resources off to someone else, somewhere else. That someone already has their own local resources and has no right to ours.

The resources God has distributed include time, attention, labor, money, and decision-making power. When we send those off to anyone else or any organization we also transfer our responsibility and accountability to the recipient. The burden is off our shoulders and now we have someone to blame or praise for the results. We become critics and spectators.

God does not allow us to offload responsibility and accountability to others because any capacity we don't use we start to lose.

Day 147

When prominent people ask us to send resources to them so they can aggregate them into a huge force they can use against others and their ideas, we stop. We can see the inevitable ethical violations this transfer of resources will set in motion. Aggregations invite aggression. Forming a huge army to attack another group frightens that group and provokes them to also prepare for war, whereas otherwise they would not have done so.

A large aggregation of resources will also cause envy and lust. Such a pile of riches attracts parasites - greedy, cunning people who want to live well off the labor and resources of others. Those who manage resources collected from far and wide end up with so much they don't worry about wasting resources, so they do.

God has taught us there is no waste in nature. Rather, in nature resources recycle repeatedly. We won't be part of wasting what God distributed so all of creation could thrive.

Day 148

Most dangerous of all, we see that large aggregations of material and human resources attract those determined to impose their selfish will on others. It is just a matter of time until a power-hungry person finds a way to gather up all the large aggregations into a mega- aggregation powerful enough to control and exploit the lives of millions.

When two megalomaniacs find their goals in conflict, they initiate devasting mega-conflicts. All life on earth suffers and much of it may well not survive.

God will not hold us innocent if we were complicit in these crimes. That is the ultimate reason we won't entrust to others the resources God entrusted to us. If we do, we end up responsible for something we have no control over and for terrible outcomes we had no power to prevent. That is a recipe for madness.

God would never cook up such a mess.

Day 149

The evils of unnecessary, pre-mature aggregation have bedeviled humanity and ravaged nature since the first village was formed.

It is not our way. We hold on tightly to our local resources and remain responsible and accountable to God and to each other for how we use them.

We have learned the ethics of the trees. Bigger is not better, faster is not better, more is not better, easier is not better.

Under God's rule better is better.

Better is seen in the quality of the relationships between lives which shows in the quality of the solutions they create and maintain together.

Better has what it takes to live on into the future. None of those other notions of "better" have the quality of living that can last.

Day 150

We make the most of the time, attention, talents, and money God placed in our hands locally to create justice where we are locally. In this way we can address a problem as soon as it shows up, while it is small and easy to correct. We make daily corrections through our daily contact with God, learning from nature, and by reasoning with each other using facts we can confirm together.

We have no need to quickly default to the bigger faster solution. We are patient. We have learned a slower, smaller, more ingenious, more unique solution will emerge. It will be effective and efficient. It will be easily adaptable. It will serve the purposes of God and support the processes of life.

Day 151

To survive, at some point humans must leave behind all substitutes, go-betweens, dead gods, short-cuts, and visions of collective glory. Instead, we must seek God directly and individually. Once quiet and alone, we must do the real work of repentance by ourselves, for ourselves until we can respond ethically and practically in our unique situation, one day at a time.

This process alone can regenerate what we lost when we severed ourselves from nature and go on to re-integrate us back into nature. No other human can tell us exactly what that will require or let us off the hook when we don't do what life requires. Along the way we learn about a short cut others are taking. It is a human production, complete with moving words, elegant aesthetics, impressive architecture, and mood-altering music, claiming to connect us to God. behaviors. It is a landmark; one we note and pass on by.

We know we won't meet God there because as soothing and inspiring as pageantry can be, it doesn't do enough to identify and remove the current key log blocking the rule of God in our lives and through our lives into our situation. It leaves us thinking we are farther along than we are. All it takes to leave something undone is to believe someone else has done it for us.

Instead, we seek quiet solitude, we learn from nature, we cry out to God and listen, ready to hear and respond.

Day 152

Any powerful compound has a half-life. For example, it takes maybe 10 minutes to drink a cup of coffee. It takes 5 hours for its effect to wear off – 30 times as long as it took to ingest it. The grip of dead gods has a half-life. If we soaked our minds in false representations of God for decades, it will take years to break their hold over us.

We must decide every day whether the effort is worth it. What we choose to invest our time and attention in each day reveals where our true loyalties lie.

Day 153

We don't expect the grip lies have had on us to break in one event, in some kind of magical catharsis. We don't seek a new clever technique, in a retreat facilitated by a guru. We know anyone claiming there is a shortcut is both lying and lying in wait for us and is probably trying to build a cult following.

They want to appropriate for themselves something we have, something we are not permitted to hand over to anyone but our Creator. They want to be the lifelong object of our trust, admiration, and gratitude. They want to take the place of God in our lives. In the process they will replace our old log jam with a new one.

Day 154

Once we realize nothing and no one can take the place of God, we settle down and accept the fact that learning how God does change puts us on a long journey.

We chose to invest years of daily undoing and releasing. There comes a day when depending on the living, invisible Creator feels natural, and trusting visible dead things the culture esteems feels unnatural.

The lasting change we start to see in and around our lives confirms it was all worth the effort.

Day 155

Social change agents are particularly susceptible to the idea of a short-cut, an alluring mirage promising fast and dramatic change. The idea is, 'there is a way to utopia NOW - with as little effort as possible!"

Typically, the argument is that the market will solve our problems through a magical invisible hand - or the mob, in the form of a majority, will solve our problems by wielding the lethal power of the state against anyone who disagrees. Bribe people and/or scare people and voila! Our future is secured, and with it a lifetime position of power and prestige for those who made it happen.

At the core of short-cut thinking is the value system of a haggler in the market – gain as much as you can as cheaply as possible, then turn around and sell it for as much as you can, as fast as you can, for as long as you can, to as many as you can.

Day 156

The haggler's strategy is simple: tell your supplier their product is not worth much. Cheat those who produce the product out of the fair value of their labor. Never think about the suffering this causes for the workers and their families. Add your "magic" to the mix, then turn around and tell your customers the final product will change their lives. Make your living by telling lies that harm both your suppliers and your customers. Laugh all the way to the bank. Live in smug luxury. Hob nob with others who did the same thing. Give each other permission to be ever more clever, insatiable, and cruel. Find and pay elite intellectuals who will argue convincingly that suspending God's ethical imperative is unfortunate, yes, but necessary to foster innovation and prosperity. Talk vaguely about the "greater good." Don't worry about God's opinion or reaction. The intellectuals assure the hagglers there is no God anyway.

Haggling is how an oppressive ruling class is born, how it sustains itself and passes its stolen power to its children who are rarely ethical or competent, but even more insatiable. The main thing is to keep it in the family.

Day 157

We do not envy, admire, or emulate clever schemers and hagglers who promise short-cuts to well-being that avoid repentance. Their path leads to extinction.

There is no haggling with God. God does not haggle with us. God does not support clever schemes to lower the cost of doing business with God to the cheapest level possible, while getting the biggest payoff possible.

We are not equals with God. Only God can change the world and bring a broad and lasting justice to all creatures on earth. God sets the terms to participate, and humans either meet them, or go extinct. It is that simple.

God is deadly serious about how we manage the miracle of life on earth. It is not ours to do with as we please. What is at stake is way beyond any personal life, any national dream, or the fate of any one species.

We don't negotiate with God or trust anyone who claims to negotiate on our behalf with God.

Instead, we learn on our own to understand God's priorities and limits, which when honored, cultivate the fullness of life on earth.

Then we learn from direct personal experience what it takes to uphold God's priorities while staying within God's limits.

There is a margin of error while we learn, but there is no second chance if we refuse to learn. There is no time to catch up if we wasted our lives learning the priorities and limits of a doomed civilization.

Day 158

After much trial and error, we finally realize something central to the way we God made us. We find we can't enact God's priorities on our own. Without daily, direct, corrective contact with God, informed by the models of nature, our efforts come to nothing. Without God, we do things we know we shouldn't do and can't stop. Without God we don't do things we know we should do, planning to get around to them later. Later never comes.

It turns out brains only function properly with constant divine connection and correction and quickly malfunction without it. Knowledge is necessary, but insufficient to change us or our situation.

Any story of a clever founder haggling with God to make the terms of participation in creation easier slanders God. The flow of life goes around and leaves behind those who think they can manipulate, bottle, and distribute God's involvement in our lives or our involvement in God's work.

Nothing turns out well for those whom life has left behind. They live and die in a dirty, shrinking, disease-filled, stagnant puddle, teeming with parasites.

Day 159

As creatures, we all share equally the right to exist and become what God intended us to become. That means we must negotiate with each other until our relationships are mutually and equally beneficial. Imposing unjust, non-reciprocal relationships by force is against the will of God.

If the relationship doesn't meet the needs of both parties, it is dysfunctional. As we keep negotiating and experimenting together until our relationship is functional, God meets us both and shows us a better way - helping us with unexpected openings in our situation.

Until we can create a mutually beneficial relationship at home, God will not help us take on anything more, anywhere else. Home is where we regularly interact with at least one other person throughout the week to solve the daily problems of life which no one can fully solve alone.

As the Scotts say...

If there is righteousness in the heart, there will be beauty in the character.
If there is beauty in the character, there will be harmony in the home.
If there is harmony in the home, there will be order in the nation.
If there is order in the nation, there will be peace in the world.

Day 160

The more we obey God the more we are fitted to participate in the work of ongoing change. We grow until we can constantly, reliably meet God's requirements for service. Only then then can we rejoin the ever surprising, ever-unfolding work of Creation.

We expect credentialling when it comes to the work of doctors and pilots, or we would not place our lives in their hands. Why would we expect anything less from ourselves in service of God? Finally, there comes a day when we accept the challenge of meeting God's requirements and chose to rise to them, rather than trying to find an easy, quick short cut around them. We embrace getting our standards from God and the struggle required to approach them in our daily behaviors.

From that day on, no two days are the same. Each day contains something new to learn and practice.

We don't find our daily existence to be boing because it is never meaningless once we have learned how to use our time and attention the way God intended.

Day 161

In God's service we focus on our duty right here, during the 24-hour term of this day. God does not promise us another day. We can't go back and undo what we did yesterday, so we live today in such a way that once it is yesterday there is little if anything to undo.

In contrast, ambitious and popular programs that solicit our local resources focus attention on a grand and glorious imagined future, allowing us to overlook or rationalize how we behave today, even if it harms another life.

Day 162

Big movements center around big personalities who seem larger than life and more accessible than God. Big movements make big promises and require no solitude. The promises fuel the intoxicated lust for increased consumption in the future, at someone else's expense, or at the expense of other species.

Intoxication is a different kind of change than the change God does. The difference is in how ideas enter our minds. Intoxication happens passively and quickly. Unlike taking in nutrients slowly through chewing and digestion, intoxication happens fast without effort. Quickly, we feel different, and often better than we did 30 minutes ago. We may start to behave differently too, and we may regret it later. The good feelings wear off, and we may find ourselves facing problems we caused while intoxicated. Now lasting bad feelings replace fleeting good feelings and our situation is no better and may be materially worse. Just because something has a quick and powerful effect doesn't mean it is good.

Mass movements function for societies the same way substance abuse does for individuals. There is no study and practice. No solitude. We are caught up in the excitement of it all, just sure there will be big, dramatic, fast changes around the corner. Thinking about the promised glorious future makes us feel warm and happy inside. We believe in the power and wisdom of the crowd. We ignore the contradictions in the movement's ideas and the unethical, even criminal behaviors of its leaders. We are taken in and taken along for the ride. We will be complicit in what the movement does, but we will have little or no influence over its actions.

Grandiose promises of rapid change appeal to our lust for more, or to our lust for revenge.

Day 163

Lust can't pass up a chance to grab and consume more than it has now. You can spot lust behavior easily - lust is incapable of waiting. When lust satisfies itself in our souls it is not long until we feel emptier than we did before. Lust always lies about how satisfying a pursued pleasure will be. Lust lies about how effective a quick cure will be.

A lust driven mind can't stand being ignored for even a minute, so it produces a steady flow of empty promises to attract people's local allotment of attention, admiration, and money.

In contrast, God's very essence is love, not lust. Love is very patient. Love waits as long as necessary to protect, give and cultivate. Love will tell the truth, even if it hurts for a while. Love will not mask a disease that needs attention. Love is more concerned about preventing the waste of a life than building a following and being liked. The mark of love is the willingness to be ignored, mocked or even hated for a long time if that is the price for telling the truth. Love will patiently use facts and logic to point out the real danger in something currently popular in the culture, or something revered in a tradition. Love will not go along to get along if an activity is contrary to God's expectations and harmful to any part of creation. Love will risk social safety now to ensure God's presence and support – the only real safety there is on earth.

Day 164

Founders of new and better eras must be free of the madness of lust and lust-gods. They must be emotionally free to patiently invest loving wisdom and disciplined action for as long as it takes. They must not live in an intoxicated state and must not peddle anything that is intoxicating. It takes serious and sober people to build a foundation that can sustain a noble effort for centuries.

It took almost four hundred years to abolish slavery as a part of the global capitalist economy. The effort was led by godly people who dedicated their lives to the effort, organized themselves locally, and passed the work on to their children for generations.

Day 165

We don't groan at the thought of undertaking a 400-year effort. It makes sense to us, given the laws of mass and momentum.

The injustices blighting the earth today took at least four hundred years to get this bad. We would be delusional to think we will overcome them in less time than they took to form. We don't expect to solve the problem in our lifetime nor seek recognition for just promising to do it someday.

We would waste time and energy on activities that make no difference if we focused on achieving the final goal and getting the credit before we die. Instead, we just set about the work given to us.

We go from trying to get as much attention as possible to giving as much attention as possible to the situation God placed us in and the needs of the lives we find there.

We shift our concern from being *interesting to* others to being fully *interested in* the problems we feel called to solve.

Day 166

To join a work of justice that may well take four hundred years to succeed, God changes us from structuring our lives around maximum consumption to lives of maximum absorption. We go from making our lives as large as possible to making our lives as efficient as possible, wasting nothing God provides along the way.

God changes our relationship to external resources until we can live simply while being happier than we were when we needed to drag a mountain of comforts after us to feel OK.

Day 167

To sustain a work that will take a lifetime, we can't burn through our supplies. God teaches us to find the maximum meaning in everything we experience along the way, rather than filling our days with an insatiable quest for increasingly shallow, repetitive experiences.

We learn to glean more from what God put in our situation rather than trying to fill our situation with more.

We stop expecting the market and the state to adapt the environment to us, so we can be more comfortable. We learn instead to adapt our lives to our environment, so life can flourish right where we are using the resources already at hand.

We learn we can live well in the situation as it is, learn from it and enrich it, increasing the stock of shared happiness in our corner of the earth.

Day 168

We discover to our surprise a refreshing freedom and lightness in this kind of migratory, frontier, innovative living. We find this is the rightful place where humans meet God, in the changing, emerging, ambiguous, indefinite space where the known and tried becomes irrelevant and no better alternative yet exists.

This fluid, undefined place holds the greatest creative possibilities. God is The Ultimate Creative Mind, so this place is the natural habitat of God, the studio where the new, natural next will come together.

By living lightly and receptively, with contentment, gratitude, and anticipation, we can approach the threshold of the space God loves most - on one condition: we no longer knowingly harm any life around us or neglect any life that depends on us.

Day 169

A long succession of failed civilizations built themselves to pursue a false happiness, the insatiable need for more, more, more, faster. For both individuals and society, what was the last generation's peak of happiness became the next generation's trough of happiness.

Their merchants found ways to entice people to consume ever more of everything, only to quickly find it unsatisfying. Their rulers told the people they had the right to consume ever more, to live ever safer and easier lives, only to find themselves fighting over who got more than who, and who had to pay for it. Together, their merchants and rulers created a society that was unsustainable. It became a voracious machine that consumed more than the environment could support.

We don't repeat those mistakes. We note those foreboding landmarks and pass on by.

Day 170

There is nothing wrong with meeting real material needs for a reasonable price. Those of us in business find a way to do that and stop there. We make no attempt to sell happiness.

There is nothing wrong with managing a community resource efficiently, providing something we all need to thrive but that none of us can produce on our own. Those of us who serve the public find a way to do that and stop there. We don't want our community to lose its own God-given sense of self-reliance and initiative by relying too much on outside help. We know if they don't use it they will lose it.

Self-reliant initiative directed at supporting God's type of happiness is the greatest virtue a community because it is what allows a people to find, combine, protect, and grows all its available resources. We work against God if we do anything to harm that virtue.

Day 171

In nature a thriving community builds itself out of what its inhabitants contribute to the environment, optimizing what the environment provided freely to them.

Each type contributes something useful, by doing what comes naturally to it.

Each type benefits from the growing availability of resources and protection the community provides.

Able-bodied freeloaders of any type are kept out by their own kind, as freeloading causes the community to collapse.

The growing abundance attracts new and different contributors with new and different contributions. Niches of nutrients emerge. New creatures fill the niches. Diversity increases. Complexity increases. The system becomes more sustainable because it is robust, better able to recover from a shock, has more ways to respond to change and most often, it also becomes more beautiful.

Day 172

After witnessing the wonderful beauty and productivity of a God-designed community in nature, we lose our taste for commercial and civic endeavors that aim to replace God as our source of guidance and dependence.

No matter how well intended or funded, the market, the state and the non-profit community all lack the ability to create anything approaching what God has created in nature.

When no one in leadership ever mentions God or nature, we sense that we will learn nothing about how God does change. They have banished the Creator and the model of Creation from the conversation from the very beginning. In place of God's genius and the models of nature they describe a future utopia they will build or a past golden age they intend to revive. Yet we know as finite mortals they can't predict the future.

God alone knows the design of what is coming and the purpose towards which higher complexity is working. Anyone who claims to know how it will all come together and exactly who will get what, is lying. Cult leaders claim to have *better answers* so their followers can turn off their brains. In contrast, God expects us to use *better questions* that keep insights flowing, so we remain unjammed and unstuck and fully available to life.

Day 173

Log jams are exhausting to live with. The energy we lack is our own, squandered on activities that don't really do anything. Nothing moves. Or if it does move it just slides back to where it was before. There is good news: God never intended humans to live the cursed life of Sisyphus.

What God has planned will require human energy. Nature stores energy in the bonds between atoms. Breaking those bonds releases an enormous amount of energy.

The process of daily repentance breaks the bonds we have formed between ourselves and seductive lies. The breaking process is painful, but pain can subside. Exhaustion only grows.

Once the pain has subsided, we discover we have energy available we did not have before. We put that energy under the direction of God, and it grows stronger.

Day 174

God changes us into effective change agents, using the newly released energy.

An agent is defined as someone authorized and trusted to manage the affairs of another, in their absence.

We know we can't hide anything from God. We have internalized God's values. God has taught us to fear the consequences of violating those values. We self-monitor and stop anytime a proposed action might cross an ethical limit. We fall silent and seek direction. Quietly, in time, God shows us an adjustment to our actions. God creates an opening in the situation that allows us to solve the problem before us while upholding the ethical imperative.

We are both relieved and amazed that once again it is possible to be equally ethical and practical.

Day 175

It is unsafe to trust an untrustworthy agent. In the client's absence such a person misuses the trust they gain to benefit themselves at the client's expense.

An untrustworthy agent keeps the client the dark about vital information, hides behind a smokescreen of complicated impenetrable language, soothes with assuring promises, while stealing from the client what they are supposed to protect and grow.

We can't behave that way. We know God sees everything we do and how we do it. God knows our true intentions even better than we do.

We know if we wander off and try to grab things for ourselves there will be no more divine openings. The very act of trying to grab what belongs to others declares to anyone watching that we don't trust God to meet our needs. If we behave in this way we will be barred from God's presence. Until we stop doing things like this God will not meet us, teach us, or help us. God will leave us to our own devices, and we will soon find ourselves trapped in another, even bigger log jam where others can easily prey on us the way we preyed on them.

Day 176

We have learned not to go rogue or join someone who has gone rogue.

You can tell when someone has broken ranks with God. Their smug certainty and pride give them away. They ask no questions. They don't listen well at all. They have no patience with context, facts, or logic, much less with ethical objections. They love to use words like "dominate" and "disrupt."

The ends justify the means, they say. "Yes, harming those who have done nothing to harm us is unfortunate. But harming them is necessary to make big, needed changes, if the innocent won't get out of our way in time."

Such words do not come from God.

Day 177

To be trustworthy change agents acting on God's behalf we must be attentive and perceptive, missing nothing that affects the work God gave us to do. We ask perceptive questions. We listen without interrupting because we know the divine is in the details. We ask thoughtful follow-up questions, which we could not have thought to ask had we not been listening.

These are the behaviors of empathy. Through them we learn to see the experience others are having, even if it is not the experience we are having. We learn to see the experience we are creating for others as much as is possible. We adjust our behaviors until others experience the rule of God when in contact with us.

Day 178

Just as God leads through touch and a quiet voice, we lead by meeting practical needs, kindly, with as few words as possible. We direct attention away from ourselves and onto the ethical issue at stake in the problem we are solving.

Words don't direct attention to God's presence, deeds do. We very rarely talk about God, if at all. We do talk about the wisdom found in nature. We can't help it!

Butterflies open their beautiful wings each morning to absorb the energy of the sun, to warm up their muscles so they can fly. The flap of a butterfly's wings can set in motion a series of events that lead to a change in the weather on the other side of the earth. Everything we see in nature had its start in an original and never-again repeated response to a unique combination of initial conditions.

Our own process of daily repentance is what builds creative, adaptive capacity in us and keeps it in good working order. This sensitive dependence upon God's immediate direction in response to practical problems is how we flap our creative wings. This allows the living system around us to change, recover and thrive on its own.

Day 179

Our guided, ethically limited actions connect resources in such a way that they naturally combine, multiply and multiply again to solve practical problems without harming any other life.

Cooperation breeds more cooperation. Safety breeds more safety.

More elegant cooperation breeds even more elegant cooperation.

More efficient cooperation breeds even more efficient cooperation.

More innovative solutions breed even more innovative solutions as people feel safe to release and redirect the energy they once spent defending themselves into the cooperative tasks at hand.

Day 180

All it takes is one missing slat in a wine barrel and all the others become useless, no matter how many there are or how perfectly made and fitted together. Without this one slat, the barrel can't hold anything for long. This this dynamic, known as "Liebig's Law of the Minimum" is a defining feature of living systems. For example, the amount of available phosphorus is the limiting ingredient for a community of plants. There is a minimum amount required for plants to grow and there is no substitute for it if it is missing. Without it little good can happen or last for long. With it there, there is little limit to how much goodness can emerge.

A living connection to God's wisdom is the ingredient in a society for which there is no substitute, as it is what uniquely among all human faculties can build relationships that are just. Justice is the slat in the barrel of society. Productive and peaceful diversity is a full barrel.

All other good things can be in place, but if responsive sensitivity to God's corrective ethical wisdom is lacking, justice remains a word many know, but not a reality many experience. A society without the real experience of justice will come apart at the point where its moral values conflict with its material interests. When it most needs to uphold its highest values, it will instead betray them. Justice will collapse and become meaningless, becoming something available only to the rich.

Day 181

God calls us to provide the missing ingredient that allows life to naturally thrive around us, quietly and without fanfare. Our highest interest is to see God's values enacted. Once we do that we won't have to tell life what to do. Life already knows what to do, if given the right conditions. The barrel will fill up with goodness.

God changes us until we can spot and absorb the wisdom already placed along our path. We don't demand a more exciting or glamourous assignment. Rather, we learn to live simply, consume less, slow down and carefully observe what we find in the situation assigned to us.

It is not random. There are patterns of cause and effect. There are wonders to behold. What is real is more interesting than any fantasy.

Day 182

To become useful to God, we learn to take note of details, to measure and count things. We unpack patterns. We notice ratios. We find meaning hidden in the ordinary. Most of all we see what is happening in the relationships between living beings in our world.

We document the real, we figure out logically what is causing what we see, we test our guesses. We make discoveries. We apply our discoveries logically to the situations we encounter. We try new methods and behaviors. We see new and different outcomes which change the situation we face, leaving it with more and better creative options than before.

We join our Creator in the ongoing wonder and work of Creation. There is no more fulfilling work. We find the meaning of our existence. Jaded boredom does not accompany us.

Day 183

We will inevitably come across an entrenched unjust pattern of human behavior. Usually, it will have been going on for a long time. Usually, it will have wide and deep support from many people. Look the other way, and you get a career. Confront it and you will pay a high price, so will your family.

How do we counter something that seems to have so much greater mass and momentum than we do? Don't rush in. Only fools do that. God does not commission fools.

Day 184

When we answer a call to address an entrenched injustice, we must first make sure we survive. Then we must make sure we succeed.

In that order.

We take logical steps to reduce the likelihood or severity of foreseeable failure. Often we avoid what is deadly because God intervenes and stops us in our tracks.

Only later do we realize God prevented a tragedy by withholding what we were certain we needed. We internalize these lessons. We recognize dangers earlier and act to minimize the functional damage they could cause us. We know we must stay in the game to win it.

Only then do we start to discover what can make a lasting difference.

Day 185

God is not in the business of making martyrs. God never shows up to magically assist in an act of unnecessary, badly planned confrontation. God does not send us on suicide missions.

God rebuilds us for long-term survival. We can't prevent the collapse of a godless, unnatural civilization. No one can and God won't.

Our job is to survive it together and emerge, unified and in good working order.

Day 186

In nature an alpha will place itself between its group and a predator, facing it down. But the alpha rarely sacrifices its own life. The predator knows it is just as likely to die or suffer severe injury as its prey.

With power and long honed still, the alpha faces down the predator and buys its group time to get to safety – then rejoins them later.

God's work will require the strength and bravery of skilled leaders for many years; it makes no sense to squander it.

Day 187

We aren't stupid. We don't throw our small mass directly against Evil's great mass. Like any experienced general in war, we don't put our weakness against the enemy's strength. We know the returning shock will harm us and do nothing to change their behaviors.

Such an impulsive move would show us to be both foolish and pathetic. Foolish because it never could have worked, and the failure was foreseeable. Pathetic because such failure reveals that we are not that bright, or at least not very mature.

Under God's direction, we take a very different approach.

Day 188

Seeking God's constant ethical guidance daily, when we come up against a large Evil force, we find a way to put our greatest strength against their greatest weakness. It will take time, but it is worth the wait.

Wonderfully, we often find that our greatest strength, our secret weapon, comes out of the recovery from what was once our deepest wound. We will never be the same as we would have been had the injury not occurred, but that person could not have been with others in their loss and suffering the way we can now.

The breakout solution is an application of how our own conflict with God and complaint against life turned around. God guides us to use what brought peace to our own souls to fashion something that nullifies the opponent's ability to sustain the fight, without eliminating the opponent.

This opens the door for God to touch the heart of a few who had been determined adversaries, turning them into committed allies. They know how to reach others.

God is the God of dramatic reversals.

Day 189

Once we know first-hand How God does Happiness we have a secret weapon, something worldlings lack and can't match: kind contentment.

Kind contentment is a goodness so strong it can survive deprivation, obscurity, and adversity to emerge even stronger and more capable.

In nature, it is precisely what can survive adversity that goes on to inhabit and reshape the environment.

Day 190

How do we bring kind contentment to bear?

We make use of a feature of the brain. The brain evolved to notice any clear exception from the norm in its environment. The exception may be a danger, but it could also be a resource that presents new opportunities.

We live and work among famished souls chasing cruel, blind, unresponsive lust-gods. This creates an environment in which insatiability, discontent and cunning selfishness are the norm.

On occasion one of these people may ask for our help, usually in managing something mundane. It is not the particular need we help them with that matters. What matters is *how* we help them. They sense in the way we meet the need that something is different about us. We are careful, competent, measured, and modest. We help without delay, complaint, or drama. We have no need to seek attention and social approval in exchange for our help.

Day 191

When we help it is clearly not about us. We have no need to grab and hoard anything we come across in the process.

We are not insatiable. We are content because we are well-taken care of by The Living God. In contrast, those we help find themselves abused and neglected by their dead gods at the very moment of their greatest need.

In our unique response to their mundane need others feel the touch of God, without knowing what it is they are feeling.

God leads by touch and calls with a quiet voice.

Day 192

As God changes us until we embody and reflect God's own likeness, there is less greedy impatience or smugness in our touch, and more kindness. Others see the guidance of God in how we move through our lives.

Most people either don't move at all, or if they do move, they do so in a predictable direction. Some move toward something they want, some move away from something they don't want, some move against something they hate. We don't follow any of those patterns. It is not possible to predict our movements based on greed, fear, or hate.

It gets under the skin of some of those we help, like a splinter in the mind.

They wonder, what is up with us? What are we up to? Why do we do what we do the way we do it?

Day 193

You can lead a horse to water, but you can't make him drink. What you can do is add salt to his oats and he will become very thirsty. Now lead him to water and he will drink a lot. And he will retain the water.

We move in a way that creates thirst. We move *with* God, *whenever* God moves *wherever* God moves. "With-ness" is the inexhaustible source of our happiness. Our happiness salts the oats for those around us, by making them aware of how shallow and fleeting their own contentment is by comparison.

Our kind contentment can create a thirst for God's presence and peace in a few people God is calling into service. For them, this thirst is innate, but someone needs to model the only way it can be truly satisfied.

Day 194

Having learned first how God does Happiness, we can well afford to give. We are so rich inside, we overflow. God has taught us how to live in a state of high-absorption, not high consumption. Life itself, in all its vastness, provides for us. When forces collide, it turns out we are the ones with the greater mass because we move with God and nature.

Meeting us is not unlike swimming in the ocean and suddenly touching a gentle, passing blue whale. We come from a different place, fuel ourselves differently and are headed to a different place. All of it is from another world, another kingdom. Our kind is ancient.

Our behavior is a trait of our own kind, revealing our ancient "kind-ness."

Day 195

A spring in the desert is a direct connection to a vast and ancient underground aquifer. Clear, cold, clean water gurgling up in the middle of a sun-scorched wasteland has no need to market itself.

Word gets out, following the path of love. Someone who has found the water tells those they care about who do the same.

A kind, content soul who can gently meet a practical need in just the right way, at just the right time has the same effect. That touch creates a memory. Like a pollinator, an encounter with one of us can set off a chain reaction that would not have happened otherwise. Our way of living is physically handed on, person to person. Our way of living is handed off by example, generation to generation.

In nature, pollinators don't need to use detached, impersonal mass media to convey the information needed to generate life. Pollinators use direct contact to transfer information. Since we are part of nature, so do we.

Give it time. God controls the schedule, not us. It is God's planet we are restoring, not ours.

Day 196

A better way of doing things can spread through a network of people who already know and trust each other, faster than any program designed to apply it on a large scale.

The better way spreads by word of mouth; it sets off a chain reaction that undermines support for the flawed idea everyone has been struggling to make work. If the way of creating happiness has been failing for some time, there will be a growing appetite for something better. Genuine thirst makes water more attractive than any form of advertising ever could.

God does not do change by sending us to attack what currently exists. God does change by guiding us to become a real, living alternative to the current order that neither needs nor seeks the approval of the current order.

A functioning better alternative instantly makes the current solution look absurd by comparison, undermining its support.

Day 197

The very existence of a strong, beautiful, effective alternative challenges the legitimacy of the current offering and its claim of being the best and final option. Nothing can survive for long once its illegitimacy has been exposed.

Those who know how God does happiness provide that living, better alternative. They don't need to attack anything directly. Their continued existence is sufficient proof a Greater Mind is present; one we can directly access and follow. It is hard to be content with the familiar once we know first-hand that something vastly better exists.

In nature and history, the sources of lasting change are the ones that are slow, indirect, and inexhaustible. Sources of change that really don't change anything for long are those that come on fast, attack directly and quickly run out of energy.

Day 198

Facts are surprisingly stubborn things. I might not like the fact that gravity acts on my body as I climb stairs but that doesn't change the experience. I still must overcome gravity to get upstairs.

The lives of those who know how God does happiness and how God does change become stubborn facts in the lives of others. Stubborn facts, over time, are more compelling than the latest fads and the most sophisticated marketing. Facts always defeat failing fantasies.

Those being restored to God's design for human life can participate in restoring God's intended role for humanity on earth. As they come alive again, so does everything they touch. Once that has become an observable fact, a bell has been rung which cannot be un-rung.

Day 199

The existing order was built on a contrived story about humanity's role in the story of earth, one that makes no sense once we understand how living systems function in nature.

The existing order will collapse under its own weight. At some point it simply will not have enough energy to maintain all its previous solutions, to keep all its previous promises. It creates the very disappointment and anger that will tear it apart from the inside out and bring it down.

The existing order will rip itself apart along the fault lines of its own internal tensions, contradictions, and rivalries. When you promise "more" as the way to provide happiness someone will always feel they didn't get enough of the "more" they were promised, and that someone else got "more" than they should have.

Under these pressures, without us driving it out, the existing order will have no choice but to withdraw from ground it long ago conquered, occupied, monopolized, and exploited for its purposes, not God's.

Day 200

After its violent conquest, the occupying power redefined the notion of God to support its agenda.

The first ground we must retake is the highest – the name, the definition of the word "God." Our truly helpful actions in response to practical needs communicate by touch something of who God really is, what God does, and demonstrate how, when and where God does it.

We use more deeds than words to communicate what we know about God. Those we help will use their own words to describe what is different about their encounters with us. Their words will help re-establish God's true reputation, not ours.

Reputation is a prediction of what one will experience interacting with someone else before it happens. We restore God's reputation, and it spreads naturally, the same way anyone else's good reputation spreads - within a circle of people who know and trust each other.

Day 201

Like a forest floor after a massive fire, life will come back. After the collapse, those who know and trust the Author of life will be guided to move into the opened space and build something new, something consistent with the laws of life that effectively reintegrates humanity into what life is doing on earth.

We operate under a different authority, entrusted with carrying out the interests of the Creator, which encompass far more than the interests of one individual, group, or species.

The unfolding of creation will commence again, moving toward something we cannot foresee, but something we know will be wonderful.

Day 202

God works on an immense time scale as environments change, and species replace species. God both reveals and conceals, as is the prerogative of a Mind immeasurably greater than ours.

Unlike the vanquished conquerors, we don't require fantastic tales about the beginning or end of the human story on earth. God has given us this day, right where we. That is enough for us. Living ethically in the constant presence of God today is all we need.

We defer and follow. Wonders await; beyond anything we could have imagined. Ours is a life of adventure.

Day 203

With new beginnings come unfamiliar problems to face. We can't draw on experience to know what to do. At each point of confusing decision, we turn to the One whom we know *does* know what to do.

We cry out for wisdom. We fall silent. We listen. We wait. We gather facts. We learn with and from each other to better understand our situation. We look for patterns and watch for openings.

God meets us. God teaches us, usually by pointing our attention to how nature solves similar problems. God helps us. Something happens we did not plan or foresee. It is usually a small, subtle change in what usually happens, but it is enough to provide an opening, an opportunity to act in a new way.

We step into the opening and make the most of the new opportunity. We set up experiments, evaluate the results, and use the lessons learned to do another round until we figure out what works predictably. We find new ways uphold and expand justice for all of God's creatures, while meeting our own needs. In fact, we discover we best meet our own needs for a long time by meeting the needs of the living system we find around us.

We take care of what takes care of us.

Day 204

Even though it would be the easiest and fastest thing to do, when God creates an opening we don't rush in and fill it with a replica of what humans have done before.

Instead, we seek God's guidance and work together until we produce something new that fits the current situation. We design our new way to continue fitting its current situation as long as it lives – the way all other living things do.

To build in rigidity is to build in failure. We build in openness and flexibility. Founding work is not just getting something started, it includes operating what we built. If what we start sets up subsequent managers to fail, leaving them with a nightmare to operate, we have ignored God's ethical direction.

Day 205

To make us effective change agents, God must first change our perspective on time and how we use it. The first thing we learn is that God entrusts a given amount of time to us and it is not ours to use anyway we want. God determines how much we get and at what point we get no more. God teaches us to zoom in and be much more careful and precise with how we use each day we are given.

Each day we find there is a way to remove something real that diminishes the stock of happiness on earth and to add something real that increases the stock of happiness on earth.

God then teaches us to zoom out and take a larger time frame into consideration before acting. We search to see how similar choices have played out for humans in the past. We see the logical, inevitable consequences of choices with the help of hindsight.

We don't assume we are wiser than people in the past, we assume they were more like us than not. If their choices turned out badly, we learn to catch ourselves when we are considering similar choices now. We steer clear and look for another way.

We consider and take responsibility for the experience we are creating for those who will come after us.

Day 206

We know humans haven't really changed much over the past 10,000 years of human civilization. What is happening now is what was happening then, and vice versa. Godlessness is not really very creative. In fact, it is tiresome, always resorting to the same short list of selfish actions leading to the same list of ugly outcomes.

If you've seen one log jam, you've pretty much seen them all.

We become immune to popular fads, knowing what turned out badly in the past was a popular fad when it started.

For most of human history what was popular was not true and what was true was not popular. We assume that pattern holds today.

Day 207

When it comes to our habitual use of time, some of us act too quickly, without considering enough variables. Some of us act too slowly, missing the moment when our actions would have made the most difference. Until God changes how we do change, we tend to get similar results from these deep-seated patterns across many domains of our lives.

For those of us who act too quickly, God teaches us to slow down, take in more information, sit with decisions longer and above all – ask God for insight before we act.

Day 208

Insight is the process of coming to understand why the situation is as it is. We start to ask what is causing the results we see? How does that happen and in what sequence? If nothing grows in a particular piece of land there are reasons. Just planting more seeds, faster, won't change the fact that everything we plant there will die.

We must first understand why everything there dies before we can get a different result next year. If we think our time is ours to spend as we will, we will resist spending the time required to understand what is really going on.

Rushing to act before gaining insight is usually trying to achieve invulnerability. We want our acts to become facts before others can stop us, making us invulnerable to their objections.

Our time is a vital resource God expects us to invest to achieve a higher state of order in our situation, not to achieve personal invulnerability. We don't withhold the time needed to understand the causes of the disorder we see. It is time well spent.

If we can identify and remove the causes of disorder, God's natural order will often re-emerge before our eyes.

Day 209

We happily invest the time needed to gain insight before acting.

The result is a more complex, elegant, effective, and efficient solution, not a re-run of what we have always done and a copy of what everyone else does. We hand on and hand off systems that are a joy to manage because like every other thriving ecosystem God has made, they have many healthy feedback loops and virtuous cycles built into them.

Our work is both beautiful and functional. Each succeeding generation makes it more beautiful and more functional, benefiting more lives, and supporting more kinds of life in more productive combinations.

Day 210

Some of us use up too much time, we act too slowly, paralyzed by fantasies of all that could go wrong. Our slowness is trying to achieve invulnerability. We want to avoid the embarrassment of being corrected by the results of experiments or feedback from others.

God teaches us that our carefulness is valuable but is not ours to use just to avoid decisions and save face.

Day 211

For those of us who hate risk, once we accept that God gave us our natural carefulness and thoroughness as something to optimize, we find ways to make the best decision we can with the information we can find, fast enough to make things better.

We learn to speed up.

We learn how to take calculated risks.

We engage the situation when engagement is most needed.

Day 212

When obedience to God requires engaging an ambiguous situation before we know for sure what will work, we find that the actual situation does not resemble our dark fantasies, which have no real dimensions.

The actual situation has definite causes and effects which we can observe, measure, and often influence. The monster in our minds comes down to size. It does have weaknesses, and we do have strengths after all.

We find when we engage early enough the situation can be changed.

Those who once waited for us while watching opportunities evaporate can see something has changed about us. We are ruled differently than before. Not by fear, but by love.

This inspires the timid ones among them to speed up when necessary.

Day 213

For those of us who hate risk: in contact with God our fears come down in size until they fit the situation. Our concerns remain large enough to keep us sharp and attentive, but not so large that they paralyze us.

To our surprise, we find ourselves enjoying the process of guided, nimble engagement. It is fun. There is spontaneous laughter. We still take our work seriously, but we don't take ourselves so seriously anymore.

Day 214

Most of all, those of us who have been too afraid of life's messiness learn that when we act in the interest of justice, God actively joins the effort. We will not be alone in the situation as it unfolds. Quite the opposite.

The fear of risk is mostly about not being able to recover from losses.

Once we learn that God constantly supplies our needs, and re-supplies us after we use up resources, our fear of risk drops to a manageable level.

Day 215

As God changes the way we do change we discover that somehow there is always enough time to do what we have been entrusted to do.

Sometimes things speed up and time flies by.

Sometimes things slow down so we can see precisely what is going on. We learn not to blur two distinct situations into one. We handle each part of the problem in just the right way, at just the right time, just long enough, for just the right reason.

We can't plan all the risk or messiness out of life. We can't plan all the opportunities for new, higher order into life ahead of time. No creature can. We don't need to. We can do something far more valuable - what God created us to do.

We can become precision instruments in the hand of God.

Day 216

Under God's direction we can reduce risks down to a manageable level and then prepare to make ongoing adjustments until we get things to work well, predictably.

If we make deals with those who don't care about God's ethical priorities or borrow money from them to ensure our material support, we do so at the cost of our own future flexibility and integrity. Chains coated in gold are still chains.

We learn to our surprise that we can rely instead upon God's timely provision and retain our freedom and integrity. We find we can't control God's provision or predict how it will materialize, but it is there when we need it. God helps those who are helpful to life. We can count on it.

Repeated first-hand experience with God's provision changes how we manage our financial affairs. In our near future God will create openings that create space for a greater justice to take root. Before that happens, under God's direction, we build a life structure that resembles an acorn. It is independent, compact, self-contained, and mobile.

When the moment arrives, we move gracefully into the opening and get to work.

Day 217

What can we rely upon?

What can we hold on to for dear life, no matter what happens, knowing for certain that it is true and will continue to be true? Our answer to that question is our religion.

Religion is the human activity of holding tightly to what we decide is certain and rejecting what we decide is not certain.

An atheist is certain there is no God and rejects of any evidence to the contrary including the fact that is not possible to prove something does not exist unless you are omniscient, able to know with certainty everything, everywhere, across all of time. In other words, the atheist rejects God because he believes he is God and doesn't want the competition. There is no greater fool than the one who fools himself about himself.

A money-chaser is certain enough money will meet every need and rejects anything that limits him from getting richer, no matter who or what he damages.

The fame-chaser is certain getting enough attention will make him happy and rejects anything that might direct attention away from himself.

A scholar is certain enough knowledge will solve all problems and rejects any limits to what humans can know.

A nihilist is certain there are no certainties (except that there are no certainties) and rejects placing any significance on his own choices and behaviors, no matter who or what he damages.

A technologist is certain there is a combination of gadgets that will create a happy future for all. He rejects any limits on what we can make machines do for us, no matter who or what suffers irreparable damage along the way.

Anywhere there is certainty there is a kind of religion. We can't choose not to have a religion. We can only choose to have a religion that is sane, healthy, and ethical – a natural religion.

Day 218

A natural religion holds tightly only to observable, testable certainties. It is skeptical of anything that it cannot verify by observation and direct personal experience in one's own lifetime. It rejects indemonstrable, un-workable nonsense.

A natural religion fosters the kind of helpful cooperation we see in thriving natural systems. Among humans, helpful cooperation flows from ethics, not ceremonies.

A natural religion is one that historically has never been complicit in harming the innocent. It refuses to support or excuse anything today that could well harm the innocent.

Day 219

There are a few certainties. Not many, but enough to live well. These few certainties did not become certain because someone wrote them down in a book thousands of years ago. God set up reality so that we can check things out for ourselves, right where we are, today, to discover what we can know for certain.

We can observe and test what is most important to know for ourselves, and indeed we must. I don't sit confidently on a chair because an old book told me chairs exist and are reliable. I sit confidently on a chair because I have good solid experience sitting on chairs. Faith is not a religious word. It is a practical word that describes the feeling one has after direct experience with something reliable.

We learn we can have faith in God's provision the same way we learn we can have faith that a chair will support our weight. It makes no difference that God is, always has been and always will be invisible.

God's invisibility is frustrating at first but think about it. At one time, neither eyes nor things to see existed. God existed before sight and seeing. Why would God need to be visible to be real?

Only when we let God be what truly God is we start to become what we truly are as well.

Day 220

God's infinite intelligence is very visible in creation. Creation is the only curriculum that is equally available to all of us for free. Creation alone is enough for us to grasp our place in it all. Closely examine nature directly, for yourself. Look and see if you don't find the following things:

We see something instead of nothing. There could have been nothing but that is not what we see.

We see order and beauty, and we see ugly chaos. There could have been only ugliness and destruction, but that is not what we see.

We see a constant flow of new and different things. There could have been only dreary repetition, everything could have been static - but that is not what we see. What we see constantly changes. Components that were once not alive now combine to form something that is alive.

Once the universe did not exist. Now it does. It didn't just happen. Something caused it to exist. Even though we can't see what caused it to exist we are still part of it.

One thing is certain; we did not cause it to exist. We are dealing with something utterly beyond anything we can do.

Day 221

It is reasonable to create a space in our minds for the idea of an invisible, unknown cause that itself was not caused by anything.

We have a natural, healthy, and ethical religion so long as we seek and rely on the Invisible Uncaused Cause.

God exists and is the Invisible Uncaused Cause. God is wise, good, invisible, and present here now – so God does not need to be re-presented by a person or a piece of art.

God knows everything we do and why we do it. God knows how we treat other creatures. Creation has built into it a natural connection between every action and its consequences. That natural connection is called justice. Life bites what bites life. Life protects what protects life.

We cannot for sure know the consequences of mistreating another creature, so it would be best to be careful when we encounter one. We may be dealing with something we ourselves will need later.

We accept no mixture in our religion of the false certainties of the atheist, the scholar, the money-chaser, the nihilist, the technologist, the fame-chaser, or old religions that have been complicit in massive crimes against innocent people and the natural world. Those lies are key logs that block the flow of God's ethical, ingenious guidance through our lives.

Day 222

The list of observable certainties continues:

Creation exists and follows deep and ancient patterns of order formation and loss of order.

Creation produces and then replaces ever-new forms of life. Everywhere in nature we see amazing diversity and amazing integration. Creatures cooperate with each other, developing patterns of behavior that benefit themselves, others of their own kind, and others of a different kind.

We don't make the exception into the rule. Yes, there was a brutal struggle for scarce resources on the remote island of Galapagos. That situation is very rare in nature.

What is far more common in nature is super abundance. In the context of abundance, we see all the ingenious ways individuals, groups and species share space and resources.

This cooperative sharing itself creates more abundance. The fittest who survive as conditions change are the most cooperative, not the most selfish.

Day 223

When we find a pattern of cooperation between creatures we would be wise to be careful.

Disrupting the pattern may harm us in time.

It is best to take our time to understand the patterns of mutual benefit until we can find a reliable way to protect and enhance the connections between living things, human or otherwise. It makes no sense to harm what takes care of us.

If we require a book or ceremony to get that through our heads, something is wrong with us. Carefulness is an innate spontaneous behavior when we look at an infant, a puppy, or a delicate flower. When we are healthy, this carefulness is as natural as breathing.

Carefulness also makes us happy because we can feel our participation in life on life's terms. Carefulness and contentment are closely linked. We naturally want to repeat anything that makes us feel happy and content.

Day 224

We find our own happiness helping to grow the happiness of all life on earth.

Precisely how we do that is constantly evolving, because Life itself is constantly evolving.

Constantly finding the next new way to contribute to Life's full unfolding in our situation – that is the fun part! We accept the challenge with gusto.

Day 225

Our list of certainties is short, but we hold on to them with all our might.

Our list is short because we do not need fables, books, buildings, shrines, rituals, gurus, priests, crowds, rallies, music, speeches, or anyone famous. Those things act like a strong alcoholic drink, quickly creating elevating moods.

Unfortunately, just like getting drunk, these activities do not create elevated ethics. They add items to the list of certainties that humans cannot verify but must venerate anyway, at the expense of paying attention to the practical needs of those around them.

Those who are not convinced about God the way they are convinced a chair will support their weight require all those things to stay convinced, since reality won't support their contrived delusions.

If it is possible for us to forget something we haven't really learned it. If someone must put on a show every week to remind us to do something it isn't a real priority for us anyway. When an action is vital we need no reminder to do it because we never forget to do it.

A religion that isn't self-evident, functional, relevant, logical, and present right here, right now, in every situation is not vital. It is not just useless, it is dangerous.

Day 226

If something considered essential for a functional connection to God can be taken away by any human force - it is not essential. Rather, it is a false dependency that makes one vulnerable to extortion.

Nonessentials are like barnacles that attach themselves to a ship. The long list of unverifiable certainties adds weight and drag. They reduce buoyancy and flexibility but do nothing to draw us closer to God. You will notice those people pay to perform repetitive rituals for them every week become jaded, bored, and cynical.

It is not possible to be jaded, bored or cynical when assisting the Creator in the amazing work of creation because it unfolds through an unending series of unforeseen events.

Day 227

With God's method of making contact, we can't even approach God until we are behaving as ethically toward other creatures as we know how to, with as much empathy as we can muster.

We establish the value of something by what we are willing to give up to obtain it. How valuable is contact with God? God only allows contact with those who value that contact over everything else.

To follow our conscience, we give up whatever we must of our hoarded power, status, or stuff. Giving these things up means we stop doing harmful things we have been doing, not for a few ritual weeks – but for good.

Once God allows us to approach and stay in contact, we will be continually changed until under any conditions we behave in helpful ways when interacting with anything else God created.

We all do better when we all do better. It's just like our Creator to set up a system like that, isn't it?

Day 228

In healthcare, 95% of patients who don't speak the same language as the doctor are afraid to speak up when something doesn't make sense or feels wrong. This results in preventable tragedies. False religions use this this natural fear and create their own language used nowhere else in daily life. False religions seek to manage your relationship with God for a fee, for the rest of your life.

There is a way to spot a false religion. Notice their language. Their words are so cumbersome and weird that only an insider knows what they're talking about.

It all sounds deep and profound, but it is just a ploy to make you think you can't possibly know the Divine without their involvement. Under the influence of this gaslighting tactic you come to believe insight into God's ways is beyond you and requires more time to learn than you can spare. Since you're busy with more important things you need someone to translate this impenetrable language and tell you what to do.

The trap is sprung. A false, unnecessary, unnatural dependency has been established.

Day 229

God's infinite intelligence permeates all of creation. We observe it the behaviors of water, air, and gravity. We can put these observable essentials to practical use right now, right where we are because they exist everywhere. It is telling that humans did not contrive any of them.

We build our daily religion differently because we build on the certainty that God is omnipresent. Omnipresence means God's ruling intelligence is in everything, everywhere.

Knowing this, we naturally do our religion differently. We use direct observations and simple verbs such as grow, run, fly, sprout, watch, sing, call, hide, chase, play, listen, see, and pause.

These are all actions that are self-evident, movements you can see and experience for yourself, even as a child. Real actions are not abstractions. They are not theoretical.

They require no advanced degree to grasp or emulate.

Day 230

We don't ask anyone to take our word for it when we point out how God works. We suggest others look for themselves in their own situation to see if God's ways aren't there for all to see, test, enjoy, and emulate.

Many people have had a bad experience with the whole "God thing" but the way they approached knowing God is what caused problem. Seeking direct contact with God as we deal with any situation alters how we manage the situation from then on. Where we once had a greedy grabbing hand or an angry clinched fist we now have the antenna God built into our brains that picks up information that was always there, but we didn't register. This shift to receptive responsiveness is the is change that changes everything else.

Anything that distracts us also prevents us from establishing constant direct contact with the God we see in nature will serve only to perpetuate the problems we face.

Entertainments soothe because they distract us. Those who manufacture rituals and ceremonies are just creating another form of entertainment designed to offer apparently easier terms than God does. They spare us from doing the necessary ethical work to enter the presence of God, because they claim to bring the presence of God to us on our terms, at convenient times and comfortable settings, regardless of how we have been treating other creatures around us.

Day 231

God's character and wisdom are embodied in nature. We hold on tight to this discovery as essential. We won't stop relying on God's character and wisdom in exchange for anything offered to us that is supposedly better because it can be owned and controlled.

We hold on loosely to anything else, letting it go easily when life moves on without it.

We stay connected in a living and flexible way to what is alive and ever changing. We stretch and expand our ability to appreciate and protect ever-growing complexity. Life already has a way and is underway using it. We will always be the ones catching up and God's happiness will always be catching up with us in glorious, intimate reunions.

This stretching and catching up is the way we worship God. God isn't impressed with any other version of worship and is not present in them. Forests get us closer to God than temples because the living community of trees is already modeling what we are just now learning to do.

No building can do that and forests smell better anyway.

Day 232

How do we fit this natural religion into our busy lives?

We don't.

We start over and build our natural religion in first, then arrange everything in our lives around it, adding nothing God will not support or protect.

We are especially careful about anything that will demand the on-going investment of time, energy, and money because those are structural elements, not just passing experiences.

We have learned not to choose first on impulse, stimulated by advertising, then think about how to fit the choice into our lives.

We think for ourselves first, then choose only what makes us more useful to God and helpful to life. Our lives become simpler and less expensive because there is less to show off, protect, organize, move, clean, and maintain.

Day 233

As we continue building a life that honors God, we combine solitude and observation with careful and honest experimentation.

We face the facts about whether other lives we interact with are currently happy and thriving, nor not. If they aren't, since nature is our model, we know something is wrong. It could have something to do with our own behavior.

If we circle back and find our actions are harmful in some way, we look for errors in our thinking, whether factual or ethical. Often there are both.

Typically, something is missing that should be there and something has been added that doesn't really do anything.

In God's design there is nothing essential missing and there is no extra baggage.

Day 234

We stay loose and willing to adjust to new verifiable information. We are more concerned about what is true than what is familiar, comforting or socially esteemed.

We are suspicious about anything flattering. Anything that suggests we have arrived and are now perfect and know everything is a lie.

No long-lived species can afford to act that way.

Day 235

To participate in God's ongoing work of change we will need to work with other change agents. Collective efforts exist all over the place in nature. Working together is as normal as it is necessary. We must get good at collaboration because there are things we cannot do alone, no matter how disciplined and skilled we are.

We can't be in two places at once. We can't get two tasks done concurrently on our own, and sometimes that is what the situation requires. None of us has all the pieces of the puzzle.

God made us to need each other.

Day 236

If we are to know how God does change, it must become a natural reflex for us to skillfully combine our insights and efforts with those of others.

We will need to learn with and from each other to figure out the next new way to take care of life in our situation because yesterday's solutions will not fit today's situation.

Each time we gain a greater capacity to work together we experience a new, original, exquisite quality in our work and in our relationship.

Like the best jobs, getting to do such work together is its own highest reward!

Day 237

We form working units just large enough to take good care of the life already placed around us, and no larger.

We learn from other units, working elsewhere in situations different from ours, methods that may be useful for our work, but we don't try to copy them or merge with them into something larger. God made us different and separate for a reason. Creation requires ongoing, unique, local solutions.

Day 238

We lose more than we gain when we use contrived, unnecessary organization. The biggest loss is our freedom to act spontaneously when needed, as needed in our local situation. Chasing a bigger size for its own sake, we end up abandoning our post, chasing a mirage that promises a greater victory.

In the meantime, in our absence, the place God gave us to live our daily lives starts to die from our neglect.

Chasing an imaginary happiness through unnatural organization, we end up causing real unhappiness in the natural organization God gave us to nurture.

Day 239

There is something about having found or amassed a visible surplus that changes what a creature does with its attention, energy, and time. Big surpluses indicate the big adaptations and adjustments now lie in the past. What lies ahead is protecting the surplus from others. Feeling one's surplus threatened, violence makes sense in a way that it did not before.

Or upon seeing the surplus another has amassed, people feel envious and cheated. Feeling envious, cunning and attack make sense in ways that they did not before. These dynamics do not develop when a creature is finding enough, just in time. God's way of meeting needs is as simple as it is peaceful.

By contrast, our surpluses get us through lean times we already know are coming and give us something to trade for essentials we can't produce from the resources we find in our environment. These behaviors are natural and ethical because they are reciprocal. Those who help store up for lean times get to share in the stored provisions when those times arrive. By trading surpluses, we create mutual support with other communities we all want to maintain, plus a natural conduit for exchanging information about better ways to do things. Anything other than these uses must also foster natural reciprocity and mutual benefit, or it is dangerous.

Day 240

Large organizations quickly become just another form of surplus. They are built to do large things. Once the large things have been done, large organizations have no obvious reason to exist and become wasteful zombies.

Bureaucracies grow by about 5% a year whether they become 5% more productive or not.

Maintenance is not as exciting as construction, but it is necessary. Large organizations that now spend their energies on maintenance cannot die, but they are not very interesting anymore either, not really.

To feel alive again they turn their attention to building something again, but something that no one needs or asked for: monumental architecture.

Day 241

Huge, expensive, glorious buildings are the hallmark of every large, half-dead, unnatural, unnecessary, wasteful organization, or society.

In a dying civilization there is always a fabulous place to gather the largest crowd possible so someone can command the attention and adoration of the most people possible.

This configuration perfectly captures insatiable vanity in concrete and metal. All lust-gods demand to be worshipped in such built spaces. On stage the audience sees a mesmerizing show. What the audience can't see is what goes on backstage. Backstage ruthlessness rules. It is a contrived illusion. It is false.

What is false tears itself apart when it meets adversity.

Day 242

The Creator chooses to meet true worshipers in quiet solitude. We feel God's presence in the company of wise old trees that anchor entire living systems more than in any human crowd.

It makes sense because trees serve as such good role models for us. What they do is brilliant and just. It is invisible to the unaided eye, yet it is a complex order that will last as long as the species exists.

Humans separated from God prefer massive architecture, whether made of concrete, brick, or digital bits that can gather huge audiences. The godless value visible size and easily dismiss ethical behavior as too costly and irrelevant.

God gets the last laugh. All large organizations, including businesses, religions, nations, and empires eventually decline and disappear.

In every case the organization began its descent into oblivion while its leaders strutted before the largest crowds they ever had, gathered in the fanciest buildings they ever had.

Day 243

Equipped with a confidence in God's provision, knowing that there will be just enough, just in time, means we don't need or seek visible surpluses or massive audiences to feel good about our lives. This frees our attention, time, and effort to flow elsewhere.

God directs our attention and concern toward an invisible reality we are entrusted to protect and nurture. Justice is an invisible reality. You can't point to it as a particular material thing, but you can clearly see when it is present in a living community and when it is not.

Justice in a society is like love in a family. You can't capture it in an object, but you can see and feel when love is there and when it is not. People who feel loved behave differently than people who don't feel loved. As agents of God's rule, our attention is directed towards creating and protecting a social reality in which loving justice is expected and normal.

Creating the social reality God expects is normal for us. It defines who we are. It is just what we do around here because it is what God made us for.

Day 244

God changes our concerns and activities from centering on the currently visible to focusing on what is emerging, but not yet invisible.

What is most valuable but not yet visible is all that life on earth is capable of but has not yet created. We fit into this emerging, unfolding picture by being virtually invisible in the world. Like sleeper cells, we are a hidden, quiet people. God has placed us everywhere, in a widely distributed pattern across the earth, unnoticed.

We hide in plain sight. Living quiet, ordinary lives without drawing any attention to ourselves is the best way to survive in a society that destroys whatever reduces profit for the powerful.

We learn what to do and how to do it right where we are, with what God has provided.

What we do quietly brings alive God's rule around us and extends God's justice into our situation as it is right here, right now, forming a sturdy pocket of well-being.

Day 245

We don't need to go anywhere outside our home to practice or our devotion or put it on display. We don't have special meeting places or scheduled services.

We don't advertise our presence.

We don't post or broadcast what we are going to do or what we have done.

For good reasons.

Day 246

Stealth and surprise combine to create a unique advantage in the battle between Good and Evil, between what sustains all that is necessary for life and what takes it away.

Evil cannot help itself. It must make a big splash. It must make a lot of noise. It cannot function without getting lots of attention and praise. Evil is empty on the inside. There is nothing there. The absence meaning and joy creates a black hole that devours everything it touches, including hope.

We are not empty. We are filled each day with the wonder of God's wisdom. We don't require attention and praise, so we quietly go to work, avoiding notice and attack,

Since no one takes us or our work seriously, no one notices how far it has spread until it is too late to stop it from multiplying.

In nature, chain reactions that are hard to start become impossible to stop once they get going.

Day 247

Once three or more people have voluntarily adopted God's way of living it can stand in contrast to the ways of those who worship themselves. To the discerning eye and noble soul, there is no comparison. For them, the argument is over. Noble souls are the types needed to lay the foundations for a new civilization. What makes them rare and valuable is their intention to use their talents to foster the well-being of all creatures, not just to make themselves more prominent and comfortable.

It takes an ordinary mind to count the seeds in an apple. It takes an extraordinary mind to count the apples in a seed. Noble souls see the future in what we have been quietly building in the unique way we have been building it. They see in our way of doing things the seed of a better, radically different future for humanity and earth.

This is what the noble have been looking for and longing for.

The noble seek to serve the purposes of God on earth because divine work cannot fail.

Those with discernment can see God's purposes unfolding right where they are - against all odds. The most capable and committed know they are seeing a work only God can do, not least because it has no need to advertise itself as such.

Day 248

Before our quiet work appears in their midst, noble souls faced a terrible dilemma. There is no shortage of organizations claiming to do God's work but is always a catch. These supposed works of God charge an exorbitant entry fee and an even higher exit fee.

Organized religions require people to give up their intellectual and moral integrity to participate, just as criminal gangs require an initiate to kill someone as a proof of loyalty.

We don't require that people deny facts, believe fables and crazy origin stories, or praise nonsense to join in.

We don't require that people overlook and excuse historic and ongoing unethical behavior by our institutions and leaders to join in. God's name has been smeared in this way. These corrupt institutions were never authorized to attach God's name to what they do.

Calling unverifiable nonsense "a leap of faith" only makes it more dangerous. If an institution can convince you a fable is true it can convince you it is necessary to harm innocent lives to do the work of God.

Day 249

Requiring noble souls to compromise their intellectual and moral integrity drives away the highest functioning people, those capable of reality-based excellence. These are the very ones most needed to start a new civilization, a society built to help life, not harm life, for as long as it exists.

In contrast, we require intellectual honesty and moral integrity because those virtues underpin the work God has entrusted to us. If we stop requiring intellectual and moral integrity God will not guide our work we will create just fraud.

God's requirements are non-negotiable and bracing, but simple and entirely reasonable.

Day 250

We receive our calling when we personally experience what life is like when one of God's signature invisible realities is missing. If it is missing for us it is missing for others as well. The absence of something God wants for all lives is painful.

Pain creates an opening in our hearts.

The human intellect is hard and cold, just sure it knows best. The human heart is tender and warm, sensing something better lies beyond our abstract certainties.

Through the warm tenderness of a responsive conscience, God directs daily activities toward creating an inclusive well-being.

Our intellect catches up later.

Day 251

Think about the experience of being known and loved for who you are. What counts most can't be seen and measured yet it is more important than what can be seen and measured.

When God calls us into service, it becomes our life's work to help create, share, and protect at least one of these invisible but essential parts of what God wants for us all.

God does not call people to amass a surplus of anything people will one day envy and fight over the way dead gods do. Even before the fighting starts, huge surpluses disproportionately benefit those who control them, they do not create a thriving commonwealth of life. Once the fighting starts, more is lost than was ever gained.

Amassing surpluses that can be seen and counted destroys what counts the most – spontaneous helpful cooperation. Only later do humans realize the value of what they lost in the process.

God is starting over and will not allow us to repeat the old error of chasing the visible at the expense of the invisible.

Day 252

God is changing the focus of human civilization from achieving invulnerability to cultivating cooperation. In the history of earth there have been population limiting events that caused mass die offs.

When these events occur it is a species' ability to form stable cooperative arrangements between themselves and between other species that allow them to survive. Those that couldn't form such arrangements degenerated and then went extinct.

To change the focus of human activity, founding leaders must replace old check lists with completely new ones. A checklist is a set of conditions that, once met, predict the happy outcome we want.

Doomed human civilization builds itself on a checklist designed to deliver surpluses, control, and invulnerability. As long as humans saw more items on the list materializing, they were happy and confident in the future, knowing ease and luxury were right around the corner.

Until then, as long as there were high profile individuals or nations already enjoying all the items on the list, who seemed so happy and secure – humans could maintain the delusion that they would one day share in that kind of permanent happiness.

Day 253

Social fantasies are made of these false checklists. Like a mirage, things don't turn out the way the completed checklist predicted they would. Even the famous people and envied nations were not as happy as they appeared to be. They successfully created the impression of enviable happiness through skilled marketing and propaganda. The reality was always very different from the image.

We always romanticize what we are excluded from, exaggerating its value in our minds. Those on the inside know what all the privileges they enjoy actually cost, and the cost is very high.

Untimely deaths and suicides mark their path like potholes in a crumbling road.

Day 254

God has a different checklist for well-being. It is no fantasy. It accurately predicts durable well-being.

Founding leaders of a new civilization ruled by God spare no effort to absorb the wisdom embodied in what healthy natural systems do through careful observation. They use their observations to develop a new checklist that accurately predicts future well-being.

The checklist is non-negotiable. It is the only list of behaviors earth can support now and into the future. The checklist creates and secures justice for all of life, not just the privileged. The checklist protects what each different type of life needs to survive and thrive.

God's qualitative checklist regulates the natural tension and competition between lives and communities so that none vanish from earth. They limit each other without eliminating each other.

In God's economy, limits are good because they allow other good things to emerge.

Day 255

Social fantasies tend to darken from one generation to the next.

One standard item found in the checklist of all doomed civilizations is a fantasy of someday eliminating some rival form of life. Each group imagines how wonderful it would be if those people who are different, who think differently, no longer existed. They imagine no rival, no differences to negotiate, no obstacles, no delays in the accumulation of pleasures. Of course, innocent members of the rival group must suffer and die, they think, but it is necessary for the "greater good."

At some point all humans try to enact their fantasies, especially if their religion says it is necessary to do, claiming God endorses eliminating the rival.

Tragedy is the result.

Day 256

We harbor no dark fantasies of eliminating those who stand in our way, who disagree with what we hold dear. If their deeds are evil, justice will catch up with their choices. They will create the conditions that cause their own demise. We don't want to be around when that happens, or to find ourselves dependent upon what is doomed to collapse. We offer no aid to their endeavors because their structures cannot be saved or reformed.

Instead, we simply leave. Without warning or explanation, we walk away, leaving the uncooperative to live out the natural consequences of their behaviors.

Vengeance is God's work alone. God alone knows how to remove evil in such a way that it will never return.

Day 257

Our work is to secure the conditions of cooperation. We too have a checklist, so we largely ignore what the godless are doing and get on with our own work. The godless cannot provide working models for us, only nature can.

By our daily example we demonstrate a short list of what is good and normal to do, and a list of what is not good or normal to do. That is what it means to rule – to establish what is and isn't good and normal. By doing it, not by talking about it, we set a new standard of what is true to life and good to do.

God rules first in an individual life, in how the individual uses their attention and time. Then God rules between two or more individual lives, in how they treat each other.

Goodness is about effective problem solving. Goodness means the constant resolution of issues, finding new productive ways to relate to the earth so that we can survive and reproduce without harming each other or other lives.

In time goodness catches up with individuals and groups who seek and follow God's direction. The contrast between God's way and the old way becomes clearer and more self-evident.

Day 258

Goodness is what we call the harvest of cooperative habits that regulate how we relate to God and other creatures. Goodness is a social function and is most clearly seen in our real, in-person relationships.

Cooperative habits between two lives adds something neither life could enjoy before. Let's say there is life A and Life B. The pattern of mutual support that grows between life A and B has a life of its own, so we will call it life C.

Combining the richness of all three lives yields results that are significantly more than the sum of just lives A and B.

God's goodness is all about surprising, ever-new functions that arise spontaneously out of a social system from the interactions between the living participants in the system.

I know that's a mouthful, but it is a wonder to behold and thrilling to be part of. Once you've experienced it you won't want to go back to chasing a dead pile of stuff.

Day 259

Anything that increases the effectiveness of the living relationships between lives (cooperative patterns) is good and equips both A and B to better deal with change in their shared environment.

Anything that decreases the effectiveness of the living relationships between lives is evil, as it leaves both lives more vulnerable to the effects of a shocking, unforeseen, external event.

Evil means non-functioning. Evil is simply the lack of cooperative behavior, just as cold is the lack of warmth. Just as kindness is the giving of the self, stinginess is the refusal to give of the self to meet the need of another.

Nature, history, and our conscience (empathy) reliably guide us to learn the checklist of good and normal behaviors that increase cooperation.

These same three sources of information also teach us to avoid behaviors that will eventually destroy cooperation, starting with unnecessary hoarding.

Day 260

In nature, among social species, hoarding is dysfunctional cooperation-destroying behavior.

For humans, hoarding anything, taking out of the environment far more than one needs at the time, causes artificial scarcity, envy, and resentment.

We can be sure anytime we see someone who is getting far more than they will ever need or deserve, somewhere there is someone getting far less than they need and deserve. This includes attention.

God, nature, and the other people placed in our path require and deserve our attention.

Lavishing attention on celebrities comes at the expense of investing the attention needed to cultivate real, cooperative relationships with those who are part of our lives. The celebrity neither requires nor deserves this stolen attention and will give nothing real in return for it.

Day 261

Once hoarding becomes normal, admired, and rewarded behavior, more people will hoard more resources than they need.

The history of the earth is marked by dramatic natural events that cut off access to food, fresh water, and breathable air. When these events occurred in human history hoarding caused panic and violent conflict over dwindling resources. We would expect to read that the celebrities and the super-rich of the day opened their storehouses to share their vast horde with those in need, but that is not what they did.

Rather, they built even more extravagant homes, took even more luxurious vacations, and threw themselves and their rich friends even more lavish parties. They drove home the point that they were immune from the suffering of the "little people" they had conned and exploited to get rich in the first place.

Nothing has changed. The same people will behave the same way in our own time of crisis.

Day 262

"Content" means something contained within something else. The more we sense we are contained within God's daily care, the less we feel the need to grab and hoard resources.

Like other animals preparing for the coming winter, we too must store up for lean times, which we know will come. But we store up no more than necessary, and never at the cost of harming other lives. Under God's guidance we discover there is always a way to meet our current and future needs that is both practical and ethical.

More important than the material resources we store up, we build up an invisible bank account of trust and goodwill between us. We draw on this bank account to help each other through tough times by offering timely, skilled services. Filled up with God's kindness we freely give the competent attention those in our lives require and deserve. In time some of them do so in return and just as importantly, give the competent attention those in their own lives require and deserve. We have made it normal and natural to behave in this cooperative, generous, reciprocal way.

The wonderful thing about informed competence is that unlike a material object, you can give it away and you still have it! Your competence remains yours to use for your own needs and to give away again in the future.

In addition, you gain even more competence every time you use your competence because in each encounter you need to modify your skills by including some new information to meet the need of the moment. This process better prepares you for the next situation that calls upon your trustworthy competence.

By freely contributing informed competence you get better informed and more competent. You have built a natural virtuous cycle into your life and become a model for others who want to make the most of the abilities God has entrusted to them for the benefit of all.

Day 263

As comforting as emotional support is, in a crisis calm competence brings deeper and more lasting comfort.

Knowledge and expertise fitted to the situation provides more security than stuff, which can be stolen or burned to ash. In fact, in times of scarcity it is precisely those in possession of the biggest visible horde that become targets of scams, rulers and angry mobs.

A big surplus makes an irresistible target for rivals and enemies. Big surpluses don't produce greater peace and contentment; they produce the threat of bigger attacks. Bigger threats produce bigger anxieties and the need to be even more controlling.

When a person or nation becomes more controlling it causes bitter resentment which simmers and finally explodes in conflict.

By chasing ever bigger unnecessary surpluses humans set in motion vicious cycles that end in catastrophe.

Day 264

We create a social environment in which it is normal to become increasingly competent at something useful, and to become adequately competent at many things. Competence creates confidence, which creates self-sufficiency, which creates the freedom to live one's life as one sees fit without external interference.

We create a social environment in which it is normal to freely offer that competence and to gratefully accept the competence of others in areas outside our expertise.

We create a social environment in which it is normal to give credit where credit is due. We never deny the existence or value of a member's unique contribution to our shared well-being. When people feel appreciated for their contributions, they offer more, and often the best they have to give.

However, when competent, generous, committed members of a society feel discounted and ignored, they offer less, and often less than their best.

We confront behaviors that cause competent people to withhold their contributions. We lead by example, privately and sincerely expressing our admiration and gratitude for their contributions. We then pick the right moment to acknowledge them publicly as well, usually as part of a team effort.

Day 265

Expressions of admiration and appreciation, when they become normal instead of exceptional – increase the "third life" between two lives. This third life is the living, cooperative capacity growing between two people. Both people become more capable individually, as a free bonus.

Among us excellence, which has no fixed upper limit, is the ethic of any group of two or more who team up. Excellence becomes the normal standard for how we treat each other and the work.

As each becomes more skilled, they contribute more to the third life between them, cooperating at an even higher level. In nature, at some point the cooperative capacity of a living system grows by multiplication, not just by addition.

Cooperative capacity grows into a virtuous cycle, increasing a community's resilience and its ability to recover from loss, when accidents happen. Even the process of recovering from inevitable, unpreventable loss adds new ways of cooperating that were not there before.

Day 266

At the heart of a cooperative community is devotion to God's person and purposes. Useful devotion is different from useless devotion. Useless devotion is tender and warm, full of good intentions, but never gets around to engaging reality with all its messy contradictions.

Useless devotion seeks to leave the world and its problems and turn inward and upward. Useless devotion does nothing to grow the stock of practical happiness on earth.

Useless devotion is selfishness, especially when it expects those still engaged in the world to help pay the bills with gifts. This is why don't have monks, and don't run monasteries.

Day 267

Useful devotion is warm, acutely aware of the situation, and nimble.

We cultivate warm, tender, trusting feelings toward God. Then we go on to cultivate a sharp mind and nimble behaviors. These faculties allow us to respond quickly and responsibly to the direction humans receive only through the channel of a tender heart.

Competence is the only thing that can complete the intentions of true devotion.

We combine deep feelings with deep understanding of the world, and then build flexible skills fitted to the needs we encounter. Anyone displaying these characteristics in their own personal affairs is qualified to be one of our leaders.

Anyone not displaying these characteristics in their own personal affairs dishonors God and discredits work done in God's name. No matter how attractive or charming, we will not consider such a person for any leadership role.

Day 268

Anything that prevents the development of useful devotion to God is another key log that stops the flow of life.

Human civilization has built itself around something that redirects the devotion due to God alone - fame and fortune.

The desire for fame and fortune is the central motivating force behind every society at war with earth, societies that live deliberately disconnected from God's wisdom and guidance:

In the cult of fame and fortune, the doomed members think there is nothing worse than being ignored and nothing better than being noticed and adored.

In contrast, we know there is nothing worse than being disconnected from God and nothing better than being close to God, working intimately in concert with God.

Day 269

Idealizing and emulating any human or any human creation comes at the cost of attending to God and learning the wisdom embedded in creation. We can do one or the other, not both.

To glorify something is to direct one's attention and the attention of others to it and point out what makes it wonderful. We will either glorify God, or we will glorify something that is not God in the place of God.

Glorifying anything or anyone other than God is the founding big lie at the base of societies that ultimately destroy living systems and collapse in violence.

Day 270

Once humans decide there is any human or human creation that deserves more attention and credit than all others they have set up a rival to God in their souls. Each rival to God has other rivals to God.

The next thing humans do is fight over which rival to God will come out on top. The most horrific wars in human history have been between competing rivals to God.

The only route to peaceful cooperation is to acknowledge what is obvious: none of us and none of our creations deserve to be glorified as the best, the highest, the most important, the most trustworthy, the most deserving.

God alone deserves such an honor.

Day 271

God is invisible, always has been and always will be.

Our job is to learn to discern the invisible and move in concert with it, not to make it more convenient to follow. God does not take human form and never has. We don't expect God to be more like us so we can relate easier. That would be trying to reduce God down to fit what we can currently contain with ease.

Our job is to become more like God so we can relate more effectively to God. We enlarge our capacity to contain more insight into the mind and ways of God as encoded everywhere in nature.

There is a vast gulf between what God is and what we are as creatures. It is not a bad thing. We live and grow in that gulf. It is the gulf of unlimited creative possibility - the natural habitat of God.

Day 272

Fame is trying to make something easier to worship by making it human, and visible. Famous people and institutions provide a convenient way for humans to avoid the challenging work of relating in a fruitful way to our invisible Creator.

Worship means "worth-ship." To worship is to identify what is most worthy and give it the attention it deserves in the form of prompt adjusted behavior.

Why should it be easy to worship what is most worthy? It takes work to discern what is truly most worthy. It is easy and lazy to go with the fickle crowd's fleeting assessment of what is most worthy.

It is just as lazy to follow what today's crowd thinks is most worthy in the form of fads as it is to follow what yesterday's crowd thought was most worthy in the form of tradition.

The lazy cannot be helpful.

The problem with junk food is it fills you up, so you aren't hungry when nutritious food is offered. In the same way, anything familiar we quickly and easily fill our heads with displaces the new and unfamiliar that is harder and slower to absorb, but always more useful and relevant to our situation. We don't succumb to mental laziness.

Day 273

Rather than mindlessly follow the crowd or tradition we discern for ourselves what is most worthy – using observation, reason, and our conscience - right now, in our own unique situation.

It is precisely the work of pruning away all that is not the most worthy that makes our devotion to God so deep, and strong. Ours is not received wisdom. It is not second hand.

Our knowledge of God and devotion to God is our own. We paid dearly for it. We remember vividly how this loving devotion came into our lives, displaced what was unworthy, and went on to rule our hearts.

As with all great love stories, it is not a copy or version of anyone else's story. Its very uniqueness is what makes it so precious.

Day 274

Since we do the hard work of growing our own reality-based devotion, we are not a fame-based, fame-driven people. We don't compete to determine who will get the most attention now or in the future. We give no place to those who want to be the center of attention and "leave a legacy."

Fame and the pursuit of fame blocks contact with God just as a nuclear winter would block the energy of the sun, killing all plant life and all the lives that depend upon plants to live.

The story of fame-based societies is like a nuclear winter. For a time, they darken the sky and bring cold indifference and death. But their time is limited.

Inevitably the earth will again be bathed in light and warmth as the air clears.

We await that moment when once again the glory of God activates the wisdom God put into all life. As we wait, we prepare to be as useful as possible in that future by being as useful as possible now, right where we are.

Day 275

If our source of inspiration and guidance is not actually here, now, with us in the gritty details of our current situation, we are sleepwalking and useless to God.

On the other hand,

Once the nuclear winter is over in our own minds...

Once the key log of fame has shattered....

Once we no longer expect the famous or those who have become famous over the years to provide daily guidance...

Once we have no more desire to be famous ourselves....

Then the bond of attachment to God's biggest rival will break and release a huge amount of energy. We will use that energy to partner with God in the work of restoration and creation, undistracted, with no more divided loyalties.

Day 276

To educate means "to lead out."

Because of the half-life of big lies, we must be led out of our dependencies on anything claiming to be wiser than God and smarter than creation, and easier to access.

There are essentially useless centers of education. It has been said that a prison is an expensive way to make a bad person worse. The same could be said of many universities. If what you learn there does not fit the problems you will face after leaving school, your education was a useless and expensive waste of time.

Your education there was probably designed to make you a profitable cog in a machine, not to make you more helpful to God and other creatures.

If your education did nothing to equip you to find the ethical way to choose, then solve practical problems, the institution probably modelled the opposite in the way it solved its own practical problems.

We don't actually remember or use much of what our esteemed teachers said. We remember how they behaved to get what they wanted, then go on to behave the same way.

Day 277

There are three schools. The first school of life is the home we grew up in. The second school is some kind of formalized educational institution. The third school is the real world, sometimes called the "school of hard knocks."

If what we experience in the third school contradicts everything we learned in the first two schools, much of our education there was useless.

If the way we were led to expect how things would happen, and how people would get ahead in life is not what really happens, we were not educated, we were indoctrinated and set up to fail.

If that makes you angry, good. Just remember, anger is not God and can't guide you, it can only supply energy. Take your anger to God and learn how to use it.

Day 278

We educate our young differently.

We equip our young to respond ethically and competently (not one or the other) to what will actually happen around them in the real world. This starts with what they observe at home.

We teach our young by our own example to cultivate tender hearts, sharp minds, and complex skills. We don't outsource ethical education to any institution or sport. We do outsource technical education to institutions with a good track record of preparing students to do complex work in the most relevant and helpful way.

Our young people learn that in nature, as in our homes, real goodness shows up in helpful acts that are small, intimate, timely, and fitted to the particulars of the situation. They learn that goodness that is grand, distanced, delayed, and is supposed to work the same way in every situation, is a mirage and something to avoid.

This prevents some of the heartbreak of disillusionment that so often embitters the most idealistic young people once they enter the world of work and see how their bosses behave.

Day 279

A doomed civilization teaches its young people that technical education is essential and ethical education is optional, even laughable. Their young grow up to fill positions of power. In critical moments when they must make choices that will have consequences for generations to come, they find their technical education is useless, and their ethical blindness is dangerous.

The technically educated will always make the wrong choice because they will choose from a narrow range of options, none of which protect life and add to the stock of happiness on earth. When the technically educated must choose between their supposed values and their material interests they will toss out their "values" quickly and secure their material interests.

To the technically educated anything that leads to invulnerability is good, and anything that leaves them dependent on the goodness of voluntary cooperation leaves them vulnerable, which is bad.

Day 280

False change agents always secure their own invulnerability first, then tell others to do things that may or may not work. Their followers are vulnerable and may well incur the costs of a failed theory or grand plan. The change agents, however, have already succeeded and won't lose anything, not even a night's sleep when the theory proves to be untrue, and the grand plan fails to change anything for the better.

True experts, true change agents, share fully the risks of the ideas they promote. In fact, true change agents bear huge costs for decades, alone, using their own resources to learn first-hand what is true and good because it participates in the way life solves problems and honors God.

Day 281

We educate our young to be effective change agents in whatever situation they find themselves. This starts with how they see and approach any situation. We teach them there are two options:

One option is to limit God's range of influence and place no limit on their own behaviors. That is the option they will see others choose. God is kept within strict boundaries while humans have no boundaries, except in theory.

The second option is to limit their own behaviors and place no limits on God's influence over what they do and how they do it.

We teach our young to spot this moment of decision early and know what to do at that moment. Our young people have seen their elders choose the second option repeatedly by now, so for them it is the normal thing to do.

Day 282

Each of the two approaches to limits has its own inescapable consequences.

If I choose to limit God and refuse limits on myself, I have closed myself to God and opened myself to the norms of the culture, with no defenses. God cannot reach me, and the culture can invade and take over my life. I shut down my conscience, and it withers away from lack of use. I become hard and cold in my pursuit of invulnerability.

Since God is not present in my life, I don't experience God's direction, provision, and protection, so I must become even more hardened and invulnerable. I live with fear, resentment, and envy. I have no time for the needs of other lives.

Day 283

If I chose to limit my own behaviors and place no limits on God's influence in my life I will be open to God and oddly, I open out to the culture around me. I don't withdraw into a monastic life all day, all week. I start each day alone in a kind of monastic communion with God but then get ready and head out to school or work, carrying God's practical kindness with me.

I become warm and tender. I am receptive to what is alive around me and responsive to what I encounter. Being receptive and responsive is what makes me useful to God.

It also leaves me vulnerable to being used and injured.

The more real contact I have with others the more I know I need God's daily direction, provision, and protection. I ask for guidance and help more often, and I receive it more often. What we use more of we get more of.

Day 284

When I choose the second option for managing limits, God meets me, teaches and helps me in the most intimate, personal ways. I receive exactly what I need, which I could not have foreseen, exactly when I really need it, which I could not have scheduled ahead of time. This experience is called grace. I am amazed because grace really is amazing to experience.

The experience of grace leaves me even more tender hearted, as I am deeply touched and grateful for God's precisely timed and tailored kindness. I naturally want to share this kindness with others. I have plenty to spare because God renews and refills me every day. Living this way is called graciousness. Graciousness is a kind of wonderful, refreshing scent that lingers on those who live in God's presence.

Our young learn to practice this second option for managing limits. They come to prefer it over the first option because it is just such a rich and interesting way to live.

We stay available to help them put into their own words what they learn about building a functional relationship with God, using as curriculum whatever happens as they work their way through the normal passages of life.

Day 285

We do not have the option of not choosing. Life is sustained by choosing. We choose between options. We choose between different ways of finding options. For example, we could choose one person who makes every other choice for us. Whether it takes a religious or political form, letting others choose for us is a version of dictatorship or absolute monarchy.

Or instead, we could let the market choose what is best for us, by identifying what is the most profitable. Or we could let the majority choose what is best for us, by identifying what has the temporary support of 51% of voters.

These options for choosing what is best have been aggressively marketed by those who would gain the most from people choosing them. Yet as God's workers, we refuse to turn off our eyes, ears, and brains. We notice that despots, markets, and majorities constantly make choices that harm life on earth, which is also harmful to us. We feel grieved.

We know God is denied any place in these choosing systems. God's interests were never considered. Creation had no representative in the meetings, so creation's interests were carved up and sold off.

We walk away from these false choosing systems. We won't lend our support to what God does not support, to what cannot survive on a constantly changing planet.

Day 286

Our charge is not to prevent the inevitable collapse of godless systems, but to survive the collapse with a set of accurate maps and blueprints stored in our default values and reflexive social habits, not in documents.

In the meantime, we don't wait for the world to change. We don't wait for a bigger, stronger force than ourselves to come in and solve things, feeling helpless and singing sad songs and reciting ironic poetry until that day. We are already vitally connected to the biggest, strongest force there is.

We start right now, right where we are, with what we already have, as we fulfill the responsibilities God has entrusted to us.

We use our own internalized maps to avoid dangerous places where nothing good can happen.

We use these ethical imprints like blueprints to guide our choices 24 hours at a time so that we can build something God will inhabit, support, and sustain.

Our actions plant the seeds of a replacement civilization tuned to life on earth.

Day 287

Each morning, we review yesterday's events and our responses, seeking God's guidance on what we did well and what we need to do better next time.

We survey the coming day, bringing to God all decision points where the best thing to do is not clear. We wait, watch, and listen. Within 24 hours we are met, taught, and guided. We choose God's best, engage and follow through as instructed.

We are not bored. We are not disengaged. We are not indifferent or cynical. We are not delusional. We are not fans or groupies. We are not self-absorbed. We take care of ourselves so we can perform our duty when called on to do so, not so that we never experience any discomfort or frustration.

We embody God's rule on earth in what we love and trust the most, in what we think about and accept as true, and most of all in how we choose to behave toward other lives.

We inhabit small quiet tidepools away from the crazed crowds, but we carry in us the living stuff of the future.

Day 288

We are different if we know how God does happiness, and we know how God does change.

We have a different religion – if we hold on to tightly to God and hold everything else loosely. It all starts there.

We have a different political system – if we live together, select leaders, make choices, and work together in ways that secure justice for all the lives in our orbit.

We have a different economic system – if we make sure every life and every type of life retains access to what it needs to someday fulfill its God-given function in the unfolding story of life on earth.

If we have learned to do these things, we have come home. We become the ones who first know what it is to truly belong, to be a useful part of something true and good that will endure.

God is helping us grasp what our part is and how to do it well. We go first and leave a trail of ethical and practical solutions others can sample. Others will follow once they experience for themselves what is possible and far better in quality. Samples do not need to be large in quantity to do the job. A little proves the existence of more where that came from.

Day 289

A doomed civilization's religions, politics, economics, and educational systems are essentially parasitical in function. A parasite lives by slowly killing its host. A parasite dies when its host dies.

We are the anti-parasites. We don't kill the host, the earth. Instead, we host the host.

We don't wait for humans to stop killing the host, we start hosting the host right now, where God placed us. It only takes two or three of us working together for restoration to begin right before our eyes.

God intends the great party of creation to have a great built-in host. God placed a unique host species within, not over the rest of creation.

We are here to function as protectors, catalysts, cultivators, developers, and optimizers so that life creates and sustains more forms of life, which create and sustain more forms of life.

Our function is to work under God's direction to bring out the best in all of life, so that life on earth can become everything God has in mind. This function is needed everywhere there is life, so we have been placed everywhere, hiding in plain sight.

If we stay by God's side and on God's side, we get to witness an exponential unfolding of wonders beyond anything we have ever imaged.

The story of earth includes us, but it is not about us.

Day 290

Like a gracious and confident host at a dinner party, we do whatever we can with whatever we have to make sure all the guests are having an enjoyable time.

We don't intervene often, but when we do it is not to engage on behalf of ourselves, or to benefit one guest at the expense of another. We engage on behalf of both guests to ensure the quality of interaction between them.

If that means stopping the harmful behavior of one guest, we do so. We make sure everyone present is safe from attack.

When we engage to ensure the ethical quality of the interactions between our guests, we are acting on behalf of God, because justice between creatures is the supreme concern of the Creator.

Day 291

Working away in the kitchen, doing our duty, nothing makes us happier than hearing gales of spontaneous laughter coming from the other room.

Laughter tells us our guests are discovering they can make each other's lives more enjoyable at little to no cost.

Cooperative habits are growing between them as they exchange ideas and methods and conceive innovative solutions. Each guest learns they are better together, that there is more benefit in cooperating than competing.

Day 292

We provide each guest with the opportunity to safely practice a new behavior, giving what they have to give with no fear of losing it for their own later use. In fact, what they have to give grows more useful when they share it with others and receive feedback in exchange.

Each guest feels there is something new and good stirring within themselves and between others when they are around what we do. They know it has something to do with the way we treat everyone.

This tidepool is tiny and far from the crazed mass of hungry fish, but it is rich in promise.

Well-hosted, the earth is doing again what earth has always done, creating new and more complex forms of life.

This unfolding is the real "greatest show on earth." We wouldn't miss it for the world because the world has nothing to compare with it.

Day 293

Stability matters. Providing the right amount of stability is critical.

Too much stability blocks creativity altogether. Too little stability prevents creativity from taking its first tentative steps in safety.

Hosting the host is about providing the right amount of safe stability while something new works itself out, one wobbly step at a time.

Life needs enough stability, long enough to get started. As long as there were volcanic eruptions and meteor strikes life either didn't emerge or remained in a very simple state. Once things calmed down and cooled off, the emergence of astonishing complexity got under way.

We provide stability while people experience for themselves how God rules in us and between us, not by removing our differences, but by them bringing out and weaving them together in completely new, surprising combinations.

Given enough time, our guests come to prefer how God does change over how the world does change. They come back for more because they don't want to miss out.

Day 294

There are two kinds of stability, each with its own base. One is the stability of a static, unmoving structure, which requires a heavy, solid foundation at its base. The other kind is the stability of a structure designed to move, which requires something at its base that restores equilibrium after a disturbance, like the keel of ship.

Moving structures get stability through constant adjustment to what the environment throws at it. Constant adjustment allows the object to return to its essential function as soon as possible, while still absorbing the forces coming at its changing environment.

An airplane constantly adjusts its wing surfaces to respond to gravity, lift, shearing crosswinds and drag. The moving kind of stability seen in a bird or plane is called soaring.

At a distance you can't see all that adjusting going on. What is visible is the plane flying smoothly in a consistent direction, at a consistent speed and altitude.

Constant adjustment to reality creates graceful, purposeful motion. Like soaring, moving stability is both functional and beautiful to watch.

Day 295

As much as we admire trees and learn from their wisdom, we are not trees. We are mammals. We are a foraging, built to relocate constantly. As foragers, not hoarders, we take just enough with us to get to the next place where we find resources.

When humans stop moving, they get sick and start to fall apart individually and socially.

When humans stop moving, they get mean and start to destroy each other.

To be restored to their natural function, humans must rediscover moving stability as the basis for individual and collective lives. They must abandon the static stability promised by surpluses. Money is no substitute for grace.

Money temporarily soothes and masks the dysfunction in our species but does nothing to repair it.

Day 296

Money acts as a bad host. Imagine a host who makes the center of the party the consumption of vast quantities of alcohol. When there is laughter, it is often mean and vulgar, at someone's expense. Inhibitions drop. Ethical limits go out the window.

No learning happens. Nothing gets better. Any plans hatched at such parties only serve to harm other people's lives, those not invited to the party. To achieve more static stability for themselves, the guests plan destructive instability for others.

If money is the organizer, the force that gathered people together, we do not attend the party. We know God will not be invited and certainly will not be the guest of honor.

Day 297

Our daily habit of seeking insight, correction and direction from God produces the constant adjustment in our attitudes and behaviors required to be useful to God.

Constant ethical adjustment to the current situation creates a calm graciousness.

Calm graciousness creates moving stability. Others can count on us to be safe, attentive, and interesting, even as everything else in their world is changing, usually for the worse.

When people feel safe their strengths emerge, and their uniqueness unfolds. One unique trait can be combined with another unique trait to create something that never existed before. These new combinations open pathways of possibility into a previously blocked, sustainable future.

Day 298

Moving stability functions like a womb. A womb is both safe and nutrient rich, while the mother continues to move about from place to place. A safe place that does not and cannot move is not a safe place, because dangers can and do approach.

There are times when only a moving safe place can remain safe enough to foster life.

Gracious, moving stability makes possible the emergence of new, unforeseen, unplanned, constructive complexity. Given the chance life naturally leaps into action. We give life the chance it has been waiting for, then rush to keep up!

There are those who believe in the "selfish gene" and teach that of life is parasitic, feeding on other life. Yet trees don't. They feed on the free energy of the sun. They are anti-parasites, giving back more life.

We too are anti-parasites. To doomed worldings we appear to give more than we get back from the social system. What they don't see initially, because they have not yet had the experience themselves, is how much we are given by God every day. Well supplied, we can afford to host wonderful parties of life.

Whereas control costs a lot of money, kindness does not. It costs time, flexibility, and attention.

Day 299

We can well afford to wait as God does what only God can do.

God is our most honored guest, soon to arrive in unrivaled splendor.

We host the host. We are part of earth and live on earth. We receive our life from the earth and then return the favor. We turn around and treat the earth as our honored guest.

God did not give us our amazing faculties as humans to squander on ourselves, but to bring out the fullness of God's genius still embedded in life on earth.

Our guest is Earth and all its different residents, with all their wonderful combinations, bathed in and centered around the energizing warmth and light of our common Creator.

Day 300

The calm graciousness we exhibit as hosts fills the open place in our hearts created when God removed the constant envy, anger, bitterness, anxiety, and depression we once felt. In this newly cleared space God has grown curiosity, gratitude, confidence, and joy.

Who wouldn't want a host who exuded these emotions?

Why are we different? It has everything to do with our goal, with what we want most. Our goal is something we know will make us even happier than we are already.

Day 301

A goal is an imagined, future state that we believe will secure lasting happiness. A goal presumes the ability to know what is best, to know ahead of time how things will work out in the future.

If I set out toward my goal and find my way blocked, I will feel frustrated. If the blockage continues, I will feel anger. Anger comes from blocked goals.

If I set out toward my goal and then circumstances make it uncertain whether I will ever reach my goal, I will feel anxiety. I may get there, I may not. I may be able to stay there, I may not. Anxiety comes from not being certain we will be able to achieve a goal.

If I find my goal blocked and its achievement remains uncertain long enough, I may come to realize my goal is impossible. It will never happen so now life itself has lost its meaning. I have no reason to live. Depression comes from having an impossible goal.

Having a blocked, uncertain, and then impossible goal leads to bitterness. An angry, anxious, depressed, bitter person can only gather and host a group of people who are also angry, anxious, depressed, and bitter.

Nothing good will be hatched by such a group.

Day 302

The culture around us uses alluring imagery to sell us on its goals. The goals are intoxicating to think about. The suggestion is, once achieved, all pain will go away and there will be nothing but pleasure. We see images of beautiful happy people living in pure joy because they have achieved the goal.

The problem is, we are looking at professional actors, trained and paid to appear to have emotions they are not in fact having. They are set in surroundings of astonishing beauty. The lighting is perfect, and so is the weather. Everyone in the scene is happily cooperating to make the person at the center of the scene completely happy, with no frustration, anger, anxiety, or depression. It is all staged, none of it exists in the real world. If we believe in the image and make what the merchant is selling our goal, it won't be long until something or someone blocks access to the goal. Most often our way is blocked because someone else is pursuing a goal someone sold them! We were set up to oppose each other, not to help each other.

In fact, every goal that has ever been sold using alluring imagery, beautiful words, and powerful music, is misleading. Reality just won't cooperate. We find the goal will be blocked, uncertain and eventually impossible for most of our waking hours for most of the population.

Seeking pleasure, we end up with pain.

Day 303

The reason we are different is we have a different goal. We got our goal from God, not from the culture. Our goal is a quality of living which comes from a certain quality of interaction between ourselves and other lives. To envision what it will be like when we enter this quality of living, we turn to samples from nature, not from staged imagery. Trees are not acting. They don't stop supporting the life of other creatures around them when the camera points away from them.

Our goal is to be useful to God and helpful to Life.

We find we never go a full 24 hours without being useful to God and helpful to life in at least one specific way. No person or circumstance can block this goal. For us, anger becomes a passing state that resolves into a greater peace as we see that often God protects us from greater involvement in things that will not endure. It may not be obvious at first how to be useful to God and helpful to life, but that is why we seek God's guidance every day and especially in ambiguous situations when it is not clear what to do.

From the immediate responses we get from others it may not be clear that we are doing any good. We do it anyway. Our behaviors are not a temporary tactic to get what we want. Like the tree, our behaviors reveal what we are and what God make us to do.

Day 304

We find we never go a full 24 hours doubting God's ability to correct and guide us to find a way to be useful and helpful. When we are in the midst of doubting, we call out to God with our concerns, and we are met.

God relieves our fears in real, practical, ways using the information we gain through observation and reason. There is always a way to do the next thing God gives us to do. It is not glamorous; it is our ethical, practical duty. When we accept our duty we are met, taught, and helped. A way opens to the next point of ethical duty.

We go through perilous passages when our path takes us through times covered by the shadows of uncertainty and the possibility of harm. God always guides us through the shadows, as we cling even more tightly to what we know from experience about God's character. God is good. God does not play cruel jokes on us or set us up for humiliating failure.

For us, anxiety is not a character trait, but a temporary state that resolves into a deeply relieved, better understanding of how God does change in the real world.

Day 305

We find it is never impossible to do what God created us to do – to be useful to God and helpful to Life. Discouragement becomes a temporary, passing state. We don't stay depressed forever. In fact, recovering the energy we used to spend on anger, resentment, anxiety, and depression leaves us with emotional reserves we never knew before. Our happiness is not fragile or permanently upended by a turn of circumstances. Our happiness is strong, adaptable, and resilient, allowing us to return to peace after a setback. Depending on how big the setback is sometimes we return to peace quickly, sometimes it takes longer, just as a ship with keep returns to an upright position faster after a small wave than after a big one. But return it does.

Our happiness is a moving stability, displacing toxic emotions and keeping us upright and afloat. Despite everything, we have buoyancy unknown to those who refuse to seek direction and correction from God.

And like a hawk soaring on updrafts of rising warmer air, our happiness raises us and moves us using energy we did not supply – free energy. Our happiness is not expensive to maintain or protect.

Day 306

We too are a willing part of nature now, so we too are reenergized every day in the same way that every thriving ecosystem is reenergized every day, for free by the energy of the sun.

We don't pay any human or human institution with our time, money or attention to comfort and inspire us. We are not here to make other humans richer and more invulnerable. We are here to help life unfold into its full richness and to do that we retain control over our time, money, and attention. We don't pre-commit those resources to any other entity besides our Creator, because doing so would make us unavailable, useless, and unhelpful to our Creator and creation itself.

If we get our comfort and inspiration from any human source, what happens when that human source misleads us or dies?

The goal of being useful to God and helpful to life can never be blocked, uncertain, or impossible. We paid a high price to get past our log jam and rejoin the river of Life.

We are now free.

We will not go back.

Day 307

We won't sell our newly won freedom. Nor will we give it over to anyone or anything else. No matter what they offer in exchange, it is not worth it. If that means traveling alone for a while, so be it.

Being alone is better than being in bad company. Bad company will always put you in a position of pursuing a blocked, uncertain, or impossible goal. Bad company will put you in double binds. No matter what choice you make you lose a portion of your freedom and integrity.

Bad company is like quicksand. The only way to deal with quicksand is to not deal with it at all. Once you're in it, everything you do to get out only digs you in deeper and leaves you even more exhausted. To avoid the quicksand of bad company you will walk alone for periods of time.

But you will not be alone.

You walk with God.

Day 308

Being in good company is better than being alone.

Stay the course. Stay close to God. Stay quiet. Learn from nature. Listen, watch, observe, learn, and enact justice in your daily dealings. You are in very good company now, and historically.

Good human company will catch up with you. How will you know when good company has arrived?

In good company, conversation is not energized by vanity, complaint, envy, or resentment.

Conversation in good company is energized by curiosity, gratitude, and wonder and leads to discoveries and creative cooperation.

Day 309

Good company needs no intoxicating substance to function.

Good company does need competent participation to function.

Good company does not focus on alluring, contrived, intoxicating imagery.

Good company is not energized by consumption, but by contribution.

Good company focuses on the observable, measurable, verifiable genius embedded in life.

Good company seeks the omniscience and omnipresence of God. In good company, as each of us brings pieces of the puzzle, we discover how best to assist the genius of life, individually and in groups.

Day 310

Good company starts in pairs. Once the pair has established a stable, adaptable relationship of mutual aid another often shows up, forming a triad.

In the triad, we learn how to provide justice for all three, all the time, in any circumstance.

Justice is dying as soon as two of the three exclude one of the three, creating an outsider whose needs the other two omit when making plans. Dismissing the needs of one who is not visibly present at the moment is how evil begins.

In contrast, for as long as any two of the three reflexively remember and defend the interests of the one who is absent at the moment, justice is alive and growing. Justice is the beginning of goodness.

Day 311

A good society builds itself out of two key raw materials:

Reciprocal loyalty and goodwill.

Loyalty is how we behave when the one we are loyal to is not around to defend their own name and interests. If I am loyal to someone I speak up on their behalf when they are not around. If I say nothing when their interests are in jeopardy, I am disloyal.

My first loyalty is to the One to whom I owe everything, my Creator. My Creator is invisible and initially appears to be absent. It is my job to protect my Creator's interests in The Creator's apparent absence. I know my Creator has a vital interest in the well-being of all parts of creation.

Defending God's interests will put me at odds with those who are disloyal to God.

If I say nothing as soon as my loyalty to God might cost me anything socially, professionally, or financially, I am disloyal. I forfeit the guiding presence of God in my life and work. Yet the safety I win by betrayal is not worth the safety I lose. I discover that those who are disloyal to God will be disloyal to me at the moment I need them most.

Day 312

Goodwill is an unwavering readiness to provide aid when someone who has earned my loyalty has a need they can't meet on their own.

There are tasks that no one can do alone at all or at least cannot do well and efficiently alone. I have goodwill toward someone if am available and respond quickly when they have such a need. I am in a relationship of reciprocal loyalty and goodwill when I contribute in equal measure to our shared well-being on my own initiative.

I contribute equally without being asked or watched. I never attempt or expect to get more out of our shared life than I put into it, thinking the relationship is just another competition I can cleverly win.

The basic building block of God's emerging rule is any living relationship governed by freely chosen reciprocal loyalty and goodwill. If that is not there, nothing else of any value will survive.

Day 313

Each member of a justice-producing, justice-protecting triad typically also belongs to another working pair somewhere.

When that working pair finds a way to include another person without creating an outsider/insider dynamic, another cell has been added. God's rule naturally grows itself through this process without marketing, advertising, permanent meeting places, or exalted leaders.

Triads linked to triads linked to triads become a lattice of life, in which all participants can exchange resources and information as needed, but no more and no longer than is needed. The total energy stored in the lattice grows and remains available for larger works of justice which could support more mutual aid and cooperation.

Day 314

Under God's rule, goals, and the use of goals change. Before God removes log jams, both individuals and groups set goals and invested their hopes for happiness in the achievement of those goals. If they felt the need to sound religious, they still loved their goals then tried to use God to achieve them.

It never occurred to them that it is not our place to use God. God won't be used and won't cooperate. So, needing a more obedient god, they create a dead one that will be useful to accomplish human goals.

After the log jam, now participating in the river of life, we *love* God and *use* short-term goals - if they help us to be more useful to God.

We don't attach love and hope to our goals. We attach love and hope to God. We release goals once they are no longer useful to God and helpful to life, which is a time known to God.

Day 315

Stuck behind our log jam we lived as if we were writing an autobiography. We were writing our own stories with ourselves as the main characters. Our stories were usually a modified copy of someone else's life. Our nation's stories were typically a modified and extended version of another nation's story.

We got the idea for our self-centered stories from something the culture conveyed to us through attractive imagery. The stories never turned out the way we envisioned they would. There were unforeseen consequences for our actions. Unforeseen events intervened to upend our plans.

The stories others were dreaming about themselves eventually cause them to block our goals, or imperil them, or make them impossible to achieve. Even worse, God did show up to help as we expected. Our religions had taught us God would side with our story against the story of others, but that didn't happen.

We decided when it comes to practical matters God does not exist and lived as if there were no ultimate authority to whom we must answer for our actions.

Day 316

There is no central, coordinating, organizing mind behind all these competing stories. Instead, everyone and every group lives autobiographically, unguided by God and unconcerned about all life. Consequently, diversity is the enemy and there is no harmony. Life itself is a threat to the story. Living autobiographically leads us to live at war with life.

After clearing our log jam, God, the author of life, takes us in hand like a pen and begins to write a better story – our biography. With each act of listening, choosing, and following, we write a sentence in the story of life on earth.

We start to become part of life the more we choose to live life's way. Our story becomes more beautiful and uniquely interesting as part of life's story on earth.

A naturalist would point out that life produces things that are far more fascinating than is required to solve the practical problems of existence. Life needs original beauty and creates it in vast abundance and endless variety. As the author of life, God intends our own lives to become things of unique beauty but does not show us the design ahead of time. It unfolds in time through acts of listening obedience.

Day 317

As we learn how God does happiness we stop living at the center of our own story and start living as a part of earth's story. All subsequent changes flow from this change.

What has changed is how we expect change to happen and how we participate in bringing about change.

Our lives are no longer tedious, derivative copies of other lives.

Our group efforts are no longer merely attempts to ape and exceed what other groups have done. What God does is always new, creative, and cooperative.

Day 318

Each part of the lattice of connected triads works on something different, uses different resources and creates different solutions that produce new results.

Participating in this larger and older pattern of life, our own lives take on a fresh uniqueness that fits the situation in a way no other life could or would.

Creativity is when something new perfectly suits the situation. When this happens we find ourselves deeply moved and so do others who see it.

As we seek and respond to God's ethical guidance we discover God is a much better writer than we were, and better than the culture's best story tellers. We no longer need entertainment to soothe our boredom. We don't need intoxication to feel alive or stop feeling things we don't want to feel. We don't need to medicate the pain of envy, loneliness, anger, anxiety, or depression with powerful substances. Our own lives become fascinating and deeply meaningful.

We begin to sleep deeply and well. We wake up refreshed and enter each new day with creative anticipation. We don't want to miss the moments of unfolding tucked into any given day. We never know ahead of time when, where or how they will appear, just that they will.

Day 319

There are no paid, recognized, full-time jobs doing "God's work" in the world. We earn our living doing jobs others could do who have no connection to God. If the job itself does not harm life, if the organization or industry we work for does not have a dishonorable reputation we can make it work.

In this way we hide in plain sight as we extend the rule of God on earth. We have ordinary, everyday jobs. We exchange skilled labor for our material support. We make an honest living. We don't seek wealth without work as no such thing exists in nature.

Besides not taking toxic jobs for toxic organizations, what sets us apart is not our jobs or titles. We don't use special outfits to mark us as holy. All that does is cause people to pretend to be more virtuous than they are until the one in the costume is out of earshot. Anyone can put on a costume. That doesn't make them useful to God or helpful to life.

What sets us apart is *how* we do ordinary jobs in real time, to meet practical human needs, under real pressure. Because we work undercover, we get to see people as they really are and then see if they really change in response to how we behave, not in response to how we dress, what titles we have or what incentives we can offer.

Day 320

We make things better where we work. The first thing we do is establish our own reputation for competent integrity. We graciously say what we mean, and we mean what we say. We make and keep productive agreements.

Next, we form partnerships, working together to keep things from getting worse. Working together reveals values and ethics more clearly than any other activity besides parenting – which is itself a life's work. Working together is the activity that bonds people, creating shared history and lifelong friendships.

Working pairs come out of working relationships. By enlisting one more trustworthy person, a triad of justice can be built in a workplace off the initial working pair. It is unwise to confront a bad ethical pattern of behavior at work with less than two people openly on your side.

Once three skilled and productive workers with good reputations speak up against a practice in a meeting, others feel safe enough to speak up and oppose bad decisions and policies in the critical planning phase.

Day 321

We take ordinary jobs when and where God provides them and fill out our jobs with creative justice. In this way God distributes change agents across the earth, through the existing system of roles that someone must fill to run a society. Our jobs place us in contact with real people to influence and put us in the middle of real problems that need solving.

Our change-agent work begins in the interviewing process and continues until we move on to the next job. We are rarely life-long employees. We are typically passing through, but thoughtful people remember us and what we stood for long after we are gone. They will often say things were the best they ever were when we were around.

You see, we have two jobs at the same time. One is open, for others to see, the other is secret, between us and God. An employee's happiness at work ultimately comes down to how well they fit in and to whom they report. God fits us to the situation at hand. We report ultimately to God, the best boss there is. We get to be where the action is, where real things happen that permit new and better possibilities to emerge.

Day 322

As hosts to life, when we see an idea being born that would be useful to God and helpful to life, we incubate the idea and protected it until it can prove it's worth. We demonstrate loyalty to the one who came up with the good new idea and defend them and their idea in their absence. We demonstrate goodwill toward the innovator by standing ready to help when asked to do so.

As good hosts, when we see an idea being born that would grieve God and harm life we act decisively to withhold the support needed for a bad idea to become a harmful system. We speak against the idea in public and private meetings, using facts and logic. We don't attack the person promoting it, but we refuse to help implement the idea.

Day 323

Just as we do at home, at work we cultivate what is good and nip what is bad in the bud. The time to do both is at the very beginning when either idea is being tentatively floated. Because we stay warm and tender, sensitive to God's concerns, we can quickly detect the subtle scent of a new goodness.

We immediately stop what we are doing and pay attention. We stop talking about what we were talking about, take notice and really listen. We ask thoughtful questions to understand better. We ask thoughtful follow up questions.

We think about what we heard and find supporting resources and information that might be helpful to the innovator. We bring these resources to the attention of the noble innovator on our own initiative, without being asked.

For someone giving birth to something useful and new, our kind attention is fuel for the soul. They don't feel so alone. In us they feel the very presence and support of their Creator. We ask for nothing in return, because we are simply passing on the inexhaustible kindness God shows us, whether they know it or not.

Our support for innovators functions the same way the free energy of updrafts does for the hawk, allowing them to soar.

Day 324

There is wise efficiency in our response to new ideas at their most vulnerable stage. In terms of time and energy investment, an ounce of prevention is truly worth a pound of cure.

Encouraging a worthy idea from a worthy colleague – and stopping a bad idea from gaining support early expends less energy and produces more results than constantly managing the consequences of bad ideas already put into action or regretting missed opportunities.

We also get the reputation of cultivating new and better ways of doing the work and adding meaning to the work. Around us the most interesting things happen, drawing in the brightest and best. Around us what goes on is not merely complaining, or speculating, theorizing, jargon-speak or mechanical, mindless repetition of "the way we do things around here."

Around us what goes on is real, tangible, observable, verifiable, measurable, and eventually repeatable. Around us what happens is new, interesting, different, and better than what was happening before.

In many situations we go first and lead the way -whether we have the title of leader or not.

Day 325

We rarely mention God at work. Sometimes it is appropriate to mention God, but we don't seek ways to work God into conversations. Instead, we direct attention to what is factually true. We make what is ethical to do a priority, not an afterthought. We talk about what is most effective, practical, and efficient. We raise standards. We find ways to do the work wastes less time, energy, and material resources. We show interest in what is interesting for its own sake, even if there is no practical use in view at the moment.

When we talk like this we speak the language of God with the accent of God's kingdom, so we don't need God-talk. Accent is the most reliable way of detecting where someone comes from.

We come from a place where spending time in God's presence every morning is normal.

Day 326

The seeds of an organization's ruin are planted at its birth. In that earliest creative stage, when an idea came into the world and began to spread - something else got mixed in that was untrue, unjust, and contrary to life. In some way God's interests were ignored and replaced with something else, something not found anywhere in nature.

The way you know something was wrong at the very beginning is to look at what happened in the third generation of people who organized their lives around the idea.

If the third generation is harmful, if it chooses its material interests over its stated lofty ideals, you know there was something in its' founding ideas or the founders' choices that give permission to act this way. There is a key log in the middle of it all, a big lie cunningly wrapped in the fancy clothing of elevated language. Once the big lie becomes sacred, it can't be questioned, and it isn't.

Those who dare to question the big lie are driven out, which essentially shuts down the organization's moral immune system.

Day 327

It is typically the third generation that sells out its integrity to get money, to gain political power or to be popular. They start by driving out those among them who are intellectually honest and ethically sensitive. In so doing they begin their slide into hypocrisy and irrelevance.

By the fourth generation no one outside the organization takes it seriously as a living source of wisdom and guidance. It is ignored, or if it is mentioned at all it is as the punchline in a joke.

We don't try to fix, restore, or revive organizations like this. All the energy that would be put into fixing a sinking ship is better used getting onto a new ship. Turnarounds don't turn around for long.

Day 328

It is rare and significant when a new society's third generation gives up opportunities to bring in more money, to gain more popularity or political power because it has chosen to defend the innocent and diverse lives around them. It reveals that God's interests outranked everything else in their founders' early deliberations about how to survive and grow. Doing justice became their defining trait.

If the third generation includes and hears those who bring facts and logic to the table to argue that something must change in the way the organization behaves, you know God was honored at conception of the organization's founding ideas.

A Godly organization does not fear new verifiable information that helps it adjust its actions to the current situation. A society founded by godly people, to further God's priorities, is one with the built-in ability to constantly update itself to retain its integrity, it's practical appeal and its moral relevance in the world.

Day 329

What is the third generation?

The first generation are those who bravely break from the past and start something new. They take on the difficulties of getting it off the ground. The children of this generation grow up inside the organization and receive the benefits of their parents' work without paying the same cost as their parents, yet they revere what their parents achieved and are loathe to see it fail on their watch.

The second-generation conserves and extends what the first generation did. The second generation is composed of both the children of the first generation and newcomers who joined the organization because they like it better than any alternative.

The third generation receives all the benefits from two generations' work whether or not they contribute very much in return. Herein lies the problem. A society's moral health is not sustained by what is done FOR its people, but by what its people freely contribute in service of their highest values, no matter how difficult it is.

As enthusiasm and support for a worthy cause dwindles its leadership faces the prospect of decline into irrelevance. The quick and easy way to create fresh engagement is to increase the benefits of participation and lower the cost, essentially treating a living community as a consumer product to market and sell, which is abhorrent to God.

By this market-based thinking, the logical path to renewal runs through entertainment and marketing. Leadership passes on to the best showman, salesperson, and deal maker. This marks the point of no return, after which an irreversible rot sets in.

It is best to leave and be the first generation in a new attempt to advance God's justice on earth.

Day 330

Fifty years after a new founding, third generation dynamics start to emerge. Before embracing any idea from the past in what you are currently building, go back and see if that idea was central to any prior human endeavor. Then look to see how the leaders of that endeavor were behaving fifty years later.

If you see shady deals and ethical compromises, you have been warned. If the leaders secured invulnerable privilege and comfort for themselves while showing little concern for those with less power than themselves, you know there was something in the founding ideas that was not from God.

From the very beginning something was off. At least one commonly accepted behavior was never just, yet the community never gave more than lip service to God's desire for more diversity and higher complexity on Earth. In fact, by the third generation you will often see forced uniformity and unanimity used to achieve unity, citing something in the founding ideas to authorize harsh coercive methods.

At some point, everyone had to look alike and believe the same things. Anyone different, with different ideas, had no place in the community and was denied the community's support.

Day 331

If a new and different idea is not based on facts or is harmful and unethical, we must keep it out. We oppose bad ideas using facts, logic, and moral argument.

But if the new idea brings newly clarified facts to bear, is helpful, and even more ethical than what we were doing before, we welcome it and put it to full use. Life never stops replacing what stops working well with something that works better, something which is usually surprising and unanticipated.

Those who bring the ideas that renew us must first protest what we are doing, then reform what we are doing. They say, "that isn't true, and it doesn't work. Here is the argument against it. Let's try this new way instead. Here is the argument for trying it." They then go out and try it.

Day 332

When we see something untrue and harmful, whether it is among us or around us, we do two things: protest and reform.

If we find ourselves in a political and economic system that harms the earth and severs people from God we oppose it. We find ways to deny and undermine its authority over our lives. We start to reduce the demand for products and services the market can only provide by doing harm. In tested increments, our new ways of helping each other offer sufficient proof that it is not necessary to live completely inside a harmful system to survive and be happy.

We unlearn and relearn. We propose experiments, agree on them, carry them out quickly and evaluate the results with rigorous honesty. We repeat this process until the results are better than the results we used to get.

There are institutions that will do no more than one cycle of learning every 50 years. For passionate young change agents this is a living hell. In contrast, we do at least one cycle of learning a year, sometimes more. This is how we engage the third generation and newcomers. We don't entertain them, market to them, and sell them an increasingly irrelevant tradition or an inevitably irrelevant fad.

We never lower the price of participating; we keep it high and raise it even higher. We don't exclude newcomers who come with new facts in hand. We invite them to the table.

Day 333

The way we do renewal is better because it works. It works because it is the way of all life on earth. Our way challenges the third generation and draws in newcomers to form a new founding generation. In our way of renewal the cycle of regeneration repeats, rather than ending in a fourth generation that makes a mockery of everything we stand for.

God takes the shortest possible route to the new and better. Centuries long, torturous, convoluted, highly political battles to make even the slightest change in an institution's pronouncements and behavior is not God's way and will not have God's help.

When God moves, God moves fast, taking the route of least resistance. God moves with those who also move fast. That which God starts lasts and gets better. That which humans start apart from God, usually doesn't last at all. When it does last, it only gets worse, living a kind of zombie existence in which it isn't really alive but won't die and get out of the way of what is alive.

Our work is better because we understand the difference between principles and methods. There are many methods. There are only a few principles. When a principle is involved we say yes or no. More often we say "yes, if" and "yes, when" or "no, if" – and "no, when."

Methods must constantly change to adjust to the changing situation. When method questions are involved we say "maybe, we'll see. Let's try it. Let's do an experiment." That's how we ask life a question and stand ready for the answer.

The principles of creation never change, although our understanding of them does change, as new facts make the principles clearer. This greater clarity helps us find better methods.

Day 334

We pass along the short list of life's unchanging principles as best we understand them to date. We hold tightly to these principles and teach our young people to do the same. They too learn to say yes and no, yes if and no if to the methods and options they encounter, based on whether or not they support or defy the short list of principles.

We make it clear that any methods we use are just temporary placeholders. Our young learn to say "maybe" to methods and to propose experiments. We invite our young people to show us where our methods don't solve today's problems and to propose new methods we can try.

They are best suited to doing this because they are most familiar with the latest technology. The new methods still must apply the few proven principles of life. Experimenting is the only real learning there is because it produces the only real wisdom there is.

Aging and dying is how life makes space for new life and new forms of life. It is natural, necessary. As our methods become useless in the current situation, we hold to our principles and graciously let go of our methods to make room for tomorrow's methods, derived from well-managed experiments.

Day 335

Humans must find a functional way to relate to the past. A dysfunctional way is to say yesterday's methods will solve today's problems, so that humans should never do anything for the first time, which means no experiments. It is dysfunctional to hearken back to things that supposedly happened far away and long ago that no one can verify. Revering dusty books and imposing buildings comes at the expense of knowing God and learning what nature can teach us.

We do not seek humanly created things that will never change as a source of certainty and security. Creation has never done anything but change. Change is the principal dynamic of Creation. The Creator clearly likes change and is really good at it.

Instead, we find certainty and security by being part of what can't go away, because it is woven into the very fabric of reality at every level. We learn through careful observation to see God's design principles that have always been there. When we look closely we see these same principles operating now everywhere in everything.

We refresh, adapt, and use anything from the past that effectively imitated one of these eternal patterns to advance justice on earth. We discard anything from the past that blocked or mocked the advance of justice on earth.

Day 336

We don't start with a utopian notion of a life with no struggle, full of ease and pleasure and then throw an adolescent temper tantrum until the state or makes life fit our theory. The reason is simple. The threat of imprisonment for non-compliance only hardens the heart of those who withhold justice from others, it does not change the heart.

If the heart does not change any imposed reform is superficial and will not last. In addition, angry mobs have a bad history of harming the innocent who happened to be in the way. God is not with those who organize tantrums as a method to bring about justice.

God is with those who organize themselves quietly, locally, and voluntarily to achieve things that increase the stock of happiness all lives can count on where they live. Reform done under God's direction takes the form of smart, organic development, building on what works and trimming out what doesn't. True, lasting reform emerges from the inside out, starting with the individual heart. It emerges from the bottom up, starting with partnerships of two, and then forming tiny societies of three.

Day 337

Even the most enduring religions last between two and three thousand years.

The notions of dead religions, a thousand years after being lost to history, discovered amid the ruins of their host civilization, often seem cruel and ridiculous. From the distance of time, it is clear their sacred ideas slandered both the Creator and Creation and granted license for one group to abuse and exploit another group of humans forever. That was the point all along.

There is a pattern in the civilizations that come and go over time.

The crueler and more unjust a civilization is the more it describes God as distant and inaccessible because that is precisely how they experience God.

The kinder and more just a society is, it describes God as closer and more accessible because that is precisely how they experience God.

A people with a distant god need professional intermediaries who conduct mysterious rituals to attract and appease their god. Or they create enormous systematic theologies to explain their god and their god's rules, which would not be obvious otherwise.

Members of a cruel society believe they can bribe their god with cheap rituals or give lip service to a what is in a book and then go out and behave anyway they want. Having appeased or explained their god they believe they can act harmfully with no real consequences, because they have found loopholes in their rule book.

Members of a kind society talk with God alone. They use no intermediary; they use no rituals. They seek guidance in the book of nature. Then they go out and behave ethically, knowing if they don't they will lose the close working relationship with God that produces all real, lasting well-being. Yet they never reduce God to a buddy or personal assistant. God remains utterly sovereign and beyond them while intimately involved with them.

Cruel societies contain their dead gods within set-aside times and places they call holy. Outside those times and places, it is acceptable to act harmfully. It is all very convenient.

To live in a kind society is to walk on holy ground and live in a holy time, every day, all day, everywhere. Since God is omnipresent and timeless the entire natural world is always sacred and must be treated accordingly to live in creative partnership with God.

We can choose convenience or co-creation as our highest priority, but not both.

Day 338

The only thing we can all interact with that is everywhere and will never go away is nature.

Just as the boundary between two countries belongs to one just as much as the other, so nature is the only thing all humans hold in common, have always held in common, and will always hold in common.

Nature alone can serve as the authoritative common text for religious, ethical, economic, and political instruction. No group's book can make that claim.

There is more genius embedded in a square meter of living soil beneath a forest floor than in the past 20,000 years of human invention. It is the genius of God.

In nature there is competition, but cooperation is the overwhelmingly dominant pattern of behavior. Cooperation accounts for the diversity, complexity, productivity, resilience, and beauty of nature.

Why study and imitate the work of guessing amateurs when we can study and imitate the work of The Creator?

Day 339

Study and imitate the cooperative, creative genius of nature. This is what we teach our young to do by letting them sample, through active participation, how we manage the daily realities of life in living partnership with God. It never gets old. It is always new and surprising. Isn't that what a healthy young person wants?

The young have an innate need to explore, experiment, and map the world to find its dangers and opportunities. For the young everything is at first unknown and untried. The frontier is where the known and tried ends. It is where exploring and experimenting begins and the perfect place for the young to discover, test and apply their unique abilities.

Youth itself is a time filled with curiosity and energy, so we encourage our young people to go where our old methods cease to work or never really have worked in the first place. We cheer them on as they find and invent methods that might work better.

The frontier is often where the outlived methods of one culture can test itself against the methods of a different culture, which may be more practical and ethical.

Day 340

For as long as there is life on earth a few dynamics will always be there. Those are the things we study, protect, and integrate into everything we do.

Everything else is subject to update and replacement as new information becomes available.

Once it can be demonstrated an idea is false, once a behavior is no longer helpful to life, once a method no longer fits the current situation, we graciously release it into the river of life, making space for what will come next.

It is in that cleared out space the young can thrive. It is there that they make their unique and essential contribution and build a life for themselves in the process.

An older generation that closes the frontier to the next generation's contributions has abandoned God.

God abandons them in return.

Day 341

What is the frontier? It is where the known and tried doesn't meet the challenge of the situation. The frontier is where human existence is stripped of the superfluous. What is left is essential, the basic building blocks of a society. The frontier confronts humans again with the central questions of existence. What is true and how do we know it is true? What is good and why is it good? Who says these things are true and good? Can we verify that for ourselves? Are these answers observable, measurable, logical? Can they be tested? Can the results be replicated?

How do we figure out together what is true?

How do we achieve and secure together what is truly good?

These questions will never go away. We must answer them constantly. We work through them by ourselves, for ourselves. Doing so is what creates a frontier community that produces working models. The best minds from older stagnant communities hear about these working models and naturally want to see for themselves whether or not the stories are true.

Day 342

Like removing a log jam, there is something cleansing and energizing about returning to frontier conditions and starting over. We are the ones called and equipped to do that. We can't be happy doing anything else. We don't drink downstream from the herd because we would catch all their diseases and become hosts to all their parasites. We drink from the clean, fresh, waters of life's core questions.

Starting over is about creativity. There are two different kinds of creativity.

Primary creativity puts something into the world that has never been there before.

Secondary creativity takes something that is already there, then improves and extends it.

Responding to frontier conditions requires the skills of primary creativity. The skills of secondary creativity are not very helpful.

Day 343

Drinking lots of pure spring water was once the most reliable cure for deadly water borne diseases like cholera. Primary creativity works the same way. It starts by devoting time and attention to God's ethical guidance, informed by nature. To continue, primary creativity requires cooperation from others, the high standards of nature, and God's daily supervision.

Primary creativity starts on the frontier, on the margins of society and then moves back toward the center to influence and displace older structures that no longer work.

People from the center who have heard about what is happening on the frontier visit. Some stay long enough to study and adopt the new methods they see. Clearly they work better than what goes on back home.

Being more productive and beautiful, a better way of living does not need marketing or coercion to spread. There is something naturally magnetic about what is new, different, and better. God is up to something.

We do our part to advance what God is doing. We show generous hospitality to visitors as a sacred duty. Among us visitors have a sacred right to being treated with generous hospitality. Hospitality opens minds and touches hearts in a way no ritual can. It is our form of public worship.

Day 344

Primary creativity seeks places where what nature has done dwarfs what humans have done or ever could do.

Primary creativity often emerges among people who have lived around mountains, in deserts, in forests and along undeveloped coastlines and who love these wild places. Here nature is the teacher. Here humans can start to figure out how we can do what nature does to solve our human problems.

Primary, frontier wisdom takes what is pure and healing back to what is stagnant, polluted and toxic. Real change happens when those from a stagnant culture absorb fresh ideas discovered on the frontier. The fresh ideas liberate and energize young creative minds who are tired of endlessly repeating the past.

As William Blake wrote..

"Standing water breeds pestilence."

Real change is not an improved version of the past. Real is a break from the past, a leap into something completely new. Real change starts with rejecting the ethical compromises permeating the old ways. Without this break from the past there will be just more of the same in the future, only with more dysfunction.

Day 345

Those who practice only secondary creativity seek the herd's approval, so they drink among them and follow them downstream, drinking from ever more polluted water. They do not seek to understand nature's standards. They do not require cooperation from others or guidance from God.

The products of secondary creativity can so dominate our time and attention we never come to know God or how God does change. Secondary creativity brings change that doesn't really change anything, as it is just an improved version of what is already there.

The efforts of secondary creativity most often create a cheaper, faster, easier way to go someplace that is not worth going to in the first place, to do something that is not helpful to God or useful to life. Fortunes are made, but entire living systems are sacrificed for a passing fad. Secondary creativity starts at the center, with the privileged and moves out to the margins, trying to impose its false superiority on the "primitives."

False superiority has within it the assumption that every possible combination has been tried and the one finally adopted is "as good as it gets."

Day 346

To know which kind of creativity dominates your thoughts, look at how you evaluate the success of your life to date. If you use comparative evaluation, secondary creativity is dominant. If you use intrinsic evaluation, primary creativity is dominant.

With comparative evaluation I ask how much I resemble the success of others. Others are my standard. Secondary creativity uses the tyranny of comparison and sometimes finally creates a successful copy, but the happiness it brings is both shallow and fleeting.

With intrinsic evaluation I ask to what degree I have become what my Creator made me to be? To what degree am I contributing what I alone can contribute to the story of life on earth? Primary creativity instinctively seeks the loving guidance of God to finally create a successful original. The happiness it brings is both deep and lasting.

Day 347

Primary, frontier problem-solving absorbs the wisdom and ways of life itself. It is truly civilized because it finds ways to solve the practical problems of living together without injustice, oppression, or violence. Afterall, on the frontier there aren't many of us. We need each other in all our variety to get through tough times, so it's not in our interests to harm each other.

We live and let live. We don't demand unanimity or uniformity. We don't impose a fixed certainty on a changing and ambiguous situation. We know from our study of nature that ever-new and surprising combinations constantly appear – on their own schedule, not ours. Life serves its own interests, not ours and not the interests of the privileged.

Day 348

On the frontier people, plants and animals are not decorative objects put on display to create envy and establish social rank. On the frontier, people, plants, and animals are vital members of a community of mutual support, thriving together or not at all.

For us, cooperation, and substance matter more than competition and show. Substantive cooperation is not possible without love. Love is not a mushy sentimental thing. It is a hardy, realistic, practical thing.

Day 349

Love is faith and trust in each other, earned slowly by exchanging information, sharing power, and successfully solving practical problems. We come to trust each other's intentions when we see consistent excellence. We come to trust each other's competence when we see consistently good results come from each other's work.

I don't need to hide information from someone I love because I know he or she won't use it against me. I don't need to spend energy protecting myself from someone I love because I know he or she would not use their freedom of action to harm me or our work. I don't need to question the competence and intentions of someone who consistently produces beneficial results. All the energy spent on self-defense is liberated and can go back into creative work. We don't withhold esteem until someone wins public recognition and financial reward for their efforts. We show appreciation as soon as we see evidence of competence and good intent.

Hearing that a trusted person is working on a problem is enough to calm me down.

I can afford to take the risk of loving someone who has a long history of achieving superior results using ethical methods, whose character is defined by those pivotal moments when it was not easy or cheap to do the right thing. No one really loves a vain or fair-weather friend.

Day 350

Settled, smug, stagnant societies have high standards – for wine and furniture. And an ethic: "buyer beware – gotcha!"

We from the frontier also have high standards – for the way we treat each other and manage limited resources. We too have an ethic – "we all do better when we all do better. So glad you're here!"

Our standards are worth the effort to uphold because when we treat each other ethically we learn more from each other faster. We learn with each other more often. We have moments of shared delight as we make new discoveries together. These experiences create deep bonds of shared history between us. We use "we" language more often to describe ourselves and our activities because we include each other in our own sense of identity.

Having gained more trust in each other, we are willing to take on bigger experiments that pose bigger risks but also hold the promise of bigger discoveries.

Day 351

On the frontier it is natural to spread out and give each other space. We respect the natural boundaries between us created by our differences. We yield to each what belongs to each.

This pattern is everywhere in nature. Even at the level of acoustics, creatures share the audio spectrum. Insect calls are at the highest frequency; birds are in the middle and animal calls are at the lowest frequency. They stay out of each other's way acoustically so each can hear the calls of their own kind. Together they form a kind of symphony that changes over the course of the year and over the seasons, but each type of life stays in its own place. This is one of reasons it is so satisfying to fall silent and listen to the sounds of an untrammeled natural environment.

For many social species there is a threshold of population density that it is unhealthy to cross. We are no different.

To stay healthy and happy we don't crowd each other. We don't intrude on each other's space.

We don't drown out each other's voices. We don't deny each other's speaking time. Just as monoculture is deadly among plants, monologue kills human learning and cooperation.

Day 352

The space, safety, support, and resources we provide for each other combine to form a laboratory. In the laboratory we can each discover and combine our unique God-given talents. We gain enough confidence to propose and conduct promising experiments together.

In time our laboratory produces measurably superior results. We produce combinations that have never been imagined or tried before, yielding results never seen before. We wouldn't go back to the old way if we could!

The new and better always comes from the scrappy margins of society, not from the privileged center. That is why we stay on the frontier, where the known and tried runs out and the mystery of uncharted territory begins.

Day 353

Mystery is the place where we don't know what we don't know. It is full of primary questions, the ones we haven't yet learned to ask. We cross the threshold into mystery anytime we conduct a worthy experiment. A worthy experiment is one that helps us to understand what is really going on or to find a method that works better than what we have now.

To conduct an experiment is to ask life a question and then be willing to accept the answer without blaming each other when we don't get the result we wanted. Finding no solution is itself a valuable finding. Many ideas look promising on paper and then turn out to be unworkable in practice.

To get to better ideas, we first trim away ideas that don't work, one failed experiment at a time.

Understanding why an idea didn't work is often the insight the leads to what does work.

Day 354

As we learn our way into a new and better future, each of us takes the role that plays to our strengths and then willingly takes on our share of the chores no one really wants to do, but that must still be done. Many utopian communities failed because no one did the dishes or took out the garbage.

Someone who is constantly seeking and receiving direct correction from God will be ethical and responsible. You can count on them. Someone who is only following a theory may feel no need to be ethical or responsible. You can't count on them.

A group of ethical and competent people is best suited to creating a new and better way of life on the frontier, which can be brought back to places poisoned by ancient deadly lies.

What most often prevents renewal and reform in old societies is an ancient error that has been dressed up as a sacred truth to make it artificially permanent. The new and better way, embodied in a living alternative, can instantly expose the ancient error as an absurd lie.

For the courageous and honest few, the natural process of replacement can now begin.

Day 355

To be civilized is to solve the problems that come from living together without excluding the needs of one group or resorting to violence.

A lawless, uncivilized society....

1. Creates second-class citizens.
2. Restricts opportunity to a few first-class citizens and their offspring.
3. Forces everyone to participate in an economic system that uses the efforts of the many to pay for the luxury and privileges of the few.
4. Violently destroys the habitats of other species to provide the resources needed to sustain its economic system.

Whatever fancy theories justified these behaviors, whether religious, philosophical, or political – it makes no difference; these four godless behaviors eventually combine to cause devasting conflict. The reason is simple. A planet with finite resources cannot sustain a system that requires unlimited growth to survive. There will be a fight over what is left when the resources run out.

We refuse to endorse these behaviors as normal. We find ways to opt out and meet our needs in ways that include others and help sustain natural systems.

Day 356

God civilizes us through the changes in values and behavior that flows from our daily time along with God. We see the harm caused by our current actions and stop them. We see the harm in our potential actions and stop them before they start. We know if we can't stop our own harmful actions, we will be ineffective when we try to stop any larger pattern of harmful actions.

As we conduct experiments, we use empathy to anticipate the injustice and suffering others must experience because of our proposed course of action. Something inside bothers us even if we can't name it yet. We stop. We go to a natural place where we can observe how true complexity works. We fall silent, pay attention, listen patiently, and seek God's guidance.

We are met.

We find there is another way. It seems it was not there before, but we can see it now.

What we learned in the process of stopping our own harmful actions we can apply to stop larger patterns of harmful behavior. In a fractal pattern that we see in nature, what works at a small scale works at a larger scale as well.

Day 357

Like the symphony of sounds in the woods, God's new way to solve the problems we all face together will include, not exclude. It will open opportunity up for more people, not narrow it down to those who think and look alike. It will demonstrate our relationship to God without words. It will not try to market itself with misleading propaganda or impose it by force.

As we are civilized up to God's standards, we become agents of true civilization. We integrate differences through long, patient struggle - without injustice, oppression, or violence. We integrate human existence into the life of earth in such a way that humans and the rest of life on earth thrive together.

We use technology to buffer ourselves enough from the harm nature can do so that we can survive and concentrate our attention on the work of hosting the host. But we don't use technology to buffer ourselves so much that we no longer sense or care when our fellow creatures are suffering and dying.

Day 358

What defines humanity is the use of language and tools. At the same time humans create religion to explain their place on the earth they create technologies to interact with the earth. Technology precedes all the other humanities.

What defines our new, emerging civilization is not the absence of technology, but how we use technology. We create technology that helps us perceive and respond constructively to life in ways no other species can. In response to our skilled involvement, life unfolds in ways it could not have without us.

Creation isn't an event from the past. God never stopped creating. We exist to help. We get to see new patterns of life unfold that we didn't plan, we can't foresee, but that serve God's purposes, which are always good.

In contrast, a civilization built on harming living systems will suffer bad consequences it could foresee but chose to deny. Then it will suffer even worse unforeseen consequences that can't be ignored. We are part of the earth's struggle, so we suffer with earth as it is harmed. But we don't sit around passively and complain.

We move daily, under the command and protection of the Creator to bring real, functional goodness to bear in very particular, tangible, local ways.

Day 359

Earth is our ally in the struggle to replace a civilization that refuses God's presence with one built to make God's presence felt in everything it does.

In a new civilization, ruled by God, humanity will see to whatever creation needs. In return, creation will see to whatever humans truly need in ways that will be as surprising as they are satisfying.

Day 360

We are well provisioned. We receive what we need, just enough, just in time. We waste nothing, including time. Even when we pause- it is useful. God provides safe, quiet places to rest and recharge along the way.

We use the time and safety to repair what is broken and replace what is used up.

We need the time to repair our relationships and make them stronger than they were before. By resolving the conflicts that naturally arise from being different, our love for each other grows.

Our love for God and respect for nature grow even more.

Day 361

To go where we need to go to be useful, sometimes God takes us through perilous passages. We are particularly vulnerable during these times. We leave the safety of the familiar and predictable. We don't know how things will work out, but we are correct in sensing there is potential harm for us and those we love in this passage.

We hold very tight to what we have learned by experience about God's character. We hold tight to God's priorities and stay within God's ethical limits.

In ways we could never have anticipated God meets us, teaches us, and helps us without coddling – and provides an opening we can work our way through, for as long as we work well together.

The solutions to the problems of the passage lie in the facts of the situation itself and the new ethical responses we create.

We emerge on the other side of the passage so deeply changed we can now participate in deep change-work.

Day 362

On the frontier between what humans have always done and what we must do next to remain a functional part of earth, no merchant or bureaucrat can offer the help we need.

We learn from nature, then look to God and each other for help. We are met. We find ways to meet our needs in a way that does not cause new problems requiring even more resources to solve.

Our repeated perilous passage experiences imprint us with a trust in God and a love for each at a depth no sermon or lecture can reach.

Perilous passages transform faith from an abstraction into a kind of indefinite memory. We can't recall the specifics of how God has met our needs, but we recall that God always did, somehow, without us harming any other life. We know God will do so again in the perilous next passage. There will be a way that is both practical and ethical.

The specifics of the peril change, but the pattern of God's powerful goodness remains through it all. The more of these perilous passages we experience the more we become calm and steady carriers of God's powerful goodness in any situation we encounter.

We have become God's change agents.

Day 363

As founders of a new civilization, our top priority is not to improve and multiply good things. Our top priority is to make sure what others will improve and multiply is truly new and worth improving and multiplying.

Ours is not a work of quantity and speed.

"More-faster" work requires no contact with God and no learning from nature. The end of godless work is "less-faster," as systems come apart in a fraction of the time it took to build them.

Ours is the work of quality and duration.

We have been changed from the inside out. Now we can do better and more enduring work under God's ethical direction by using the models we keep finding in nature.

Day 364

The most important new and better thing we bring to earth is the ability to manage diversity with the wisdom God embedded in all of creation. The effective management of diversity is the missing slat in the wine barrel of human civilization, through which everything else is lost.

The refusal to manage diversity God's way has a name: hate. Hate grows and multiplies. When hate is fully grown it acts. When hate acts it can destroy in a few weeks what took centuries to build.

Throughout 10,000 years of civilization humans have proven powerless to break the wasteful pattern of boom, bust and conflict. The essence of the pattern has not changed. The only thing that has changed is the scale of devastation we can bring to each other and the planet.

Apart from God, all succeeding civilizations have achieved is the ability to destroy "more life, faster."

It is impossible to break the nullifying grip of hate without direct contact with God. Making contact with any human representation of God, or by placing our trust in any replacement for God has no proven effect on hate.

Day 365

We see nature's astounding productivity in its ability to rapidly produce new combinations of diverse components in an unending succession if there is a catalyst in the mix. A catalyst can cause a process of combination to happen 10,000 times faster than it would have otherwise, setting off exponential growth. From there, quantity and speed take care of themselves. This is God's way of doing "more, faster."

Until we share this ability to deal productively with all the differences between creatures and communities of life on earth, all our creations will someday burn to ashes in a fraction of the time it took to build them. The weapons systems we built to protect our stuff from those who are different from us will vaporize us along with all our stuff.

We will need to pay attention to learn how God does diversity until one day we can participate in Creation as effective catalysts of healthy change. God will change us until we gain the crucial ability to self-regulate. Then we can make productive use of all our amazing human abilities. If the quality of our work is pleasing to God and helpful to life, it will naturally survive and grow – exponentially.

God will use our changed lives to set off the most significant change to ever happen during the term of human life on earth. The chain reaction will create an effect that will be visible from space.

Epilogue

The journey described in this book brings us back to the function God intended for us as part of earth, the very reason humanity exists. Along the way we discover why humans were entrusted with such unusual capacities in the first place. Before repentance and regeneration, we live in contact with ourselves and get our value patterns from our culture. Once we live in a state of repentance and regeneration we live in contact with God and get our value patterns from nature, including our appreciation of how change works – when it actually works.

The statements in this book are often hard-hitting, giving no quarter for popular falsehoods that have gone unchallenged for millennia. The immune system in our bodies treats pathogens the same way. It does not make peace with what is trying to kill the body. It does not overlook what tries to live off the body's slow death. It knows how to remove those things and doesn't stop until it has. It learns to respond even more strongly the next time the threat appears.

In nature, health does not come from avoiding all sickness or injury. That is not possible. After having avoided what can be avoided, health is the ability to overcome sickness and injury - constantly and more quickly the next time.

Once the sickness is gone, once the injury is healed, the body naturally rebounds to do whatever else it needs to do to be even more alive.

There are those who, connected to God's constant guidance, can undertake this journey, and achieve true freedom from the pathogens of a sick and destructive civilization. They will use their hard-won freedom to bring justice back to earth, which is something all other species need, but no other species can do.

My prayer is that this book may serve as an accurate guide along the way for those who need it, until it is no longer needed.

Godspeed my friend.

"Where there is danger, that which will save us also grows."

- Friedrich Hölderlin

Base Camp
For those called to something higher
www.howgoddoeshappiness.com

www.ingramcontent.com/pod-product-compliance
Lightning Source LLC
Chambersburg PA
CBHW070608030426
42337CB00020B/3718